GOOGLE+™

Companion

GOOGLE+™

Companion

MARK HATTERSLEY

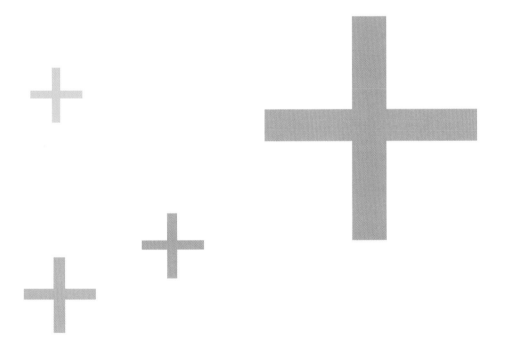

WILEY

John Wiley & Sons, Inc.

Google+™ Companion
Published by
John Wiley & Sons, Inc.
10475 Crosspoint Blvd.
Indianapolis, IN 46256
www.wiley.com

Copyright © 2012 by John Wiley & Sons, Inc., Indianapolis, Indiana

Published simultaneously in Canada

ISBN: 978-1-118-18646-6

Manufactured in the United States of America

10 9 8 7 6 5 4 3 2 1

For general information on our other products and services or to obtain technical support, please contact our Customer Care Department within the U.S. at (877) 762-2974, outside the U.S. at (317) 572-3993 or fax (317) 572-4002.

John Wiley & Sons publishes in a variety of print and electronic formats and by print-on-demand. Some material included with standard print versions of this book may not be included in e-books or in print-on-demand. If this book refers to media such as a CD or DVD that is not included in the version you purchased, you may download this material at http://booksupport.wiley.com. For more information about Wiley products, visit www.wiley.com.

Library of Congress Control Number: 2012935617

CREDITS

Acquisitions Editor
Aaron Black

Project Editor
Kristin Vorce

Technical Editor
Todd Meister

Copy Editor
Lauren Kennedy

Editorial Director
Robyn Siesky

Business Manager
Amy Knies

Senior Marketing Manager
Sandy Smith

Vice President and Executive Group Publisher
Richard Swadley

Vice President and Executive Publisher
Barry Pruett

Project Coordinator
Sheree Montgomery

Graphics and Production Specialist
Andrea Hornberger

Quality Control Technicians
Lindsay Amones
Melissa Cossell

Proofreading and Indexing
Steve Rath
Penny L. Stuart

I'd like to dedicate this book to my sisters, Vic and Wendy, for putting up with having a mad little tech-obsessed monkey running around the house. And for loving it nonetheless.

Of course, to my mum and dad; and to my grandparents: the ones still here and the ones looking after me from on high (I am still practicing my French).

As this book is about social networking, I'd also like to dedicate it to my friends, some of the best people I've ever known (in no particular order): Will, Luke, Nick, Kendall, Simon, Toby, Emma, Helen, Alex, David, Heidi, Sarah, Ben, Toni, Matt, Kate, Jenny, and Joy.

Above all to my wife, Rosemary. Thank you for putting up with me.

And to my cat, Amber. Thank you for scratching me and biting my toes. It takes my mind off work.

✛ ABOUT THE AUTHOR

MARK HATTERSLEY is an unabashed tech enthusiast who loves computers and gadgets — mostly because he's a geek but also because he believes that good technology has the power to unlock people's creativity, give them unparalleled freedom of expression, and grant them the ability to communicate with like-minded people around the world.

Mark is editor in chief of Macworld UK, and he runs a number of tech-related websites and print magazines, including *Macworld, Digital Arts,* MacVideo.tv, and *iPad & iPhone User.*

Mark is a huge advocate of social media networks, not just as a way of keeping in touch with friends (important though that is), but also as a means for disparate groups of people to hook up, organize around causes (some harmless, others important), and find common ground in the real world with people they might otherwise have never met.

Mark has seen the rise of Facebook and Twitter, and the fall of MySpace; he loves LinkedIn and was one of the first people to recognize the potential of Google+.

Mark lives in London with his wife Rosemary and their cat Amber. Now that this book is finished, he'll be found in Skyrim on the Xbox for a while.

You can follow Mark on Google+ (http://goo.gl/h16t3) and he promises to be happy to chat about tech, random things happening in the world, and the joys of pet ownership all day long (you may have to suffer cat photographs).

 ACKNOWLEDGMENTS

Thanks to Kristin Vorce for tireless copyediting, production prodding, and fantastic advice when my writing style gets out of hand. Also to Todd Meister whose sharp-eyed technical writing advice and support has made this book immeasurably more accurate. Finally, to Aaron Black for convincing Wiley to commission a book on Google+. This book would not have seen the light of day without all of you.

CONTENTS AT A GLANCE

✚ CONTENTS

# INTRODUCTION

There was a time when social networking was seen as a fun, slightly frivolous, and generally unimportant thing to do: a good way to waste time online. And it can still be that if you want it to be. But there's never really been anything that frivolous about keeping in touch with friends, family, and the world in general. Communication is one of the most fundamental parts of being human; I'm just surprised it took the Internet so long to catch on.

Social networking is the Internet with a human face. It's about real people talking about the things that are happening to them, sharing pictures and video, and above all, retelling each other's stories.

So what makes Google+ so special and why read a book on it? Google+ is a powerful social networking service that packs features many other social networks lack. It offers great potential to those willing to learn its many nuanced features. In this book, you'll learn how to manage Circles (Google+'s powerful new way to organize groups of people); how to set up really effective, eye-catching profiles; how to share movies and images that integrate with Google+'s powerful mapping and tagging technology; how to manage your privacy settings; and how to use Google+ to promote a business, brand, group, or band.

A guy in my Google+ Circles named Vago Damitio said this:

> Facebook is like college. You are connected with the people you grew up with, people from the same town, people who are in your classes — and think of classes as being the different facets of your life.

> Twitter is more like the radio. You tune into it to see what is happening, to hear gossip, famous people making sound bites, or to perhaps catch up with friends — but only in a text message kind of way.

> Google+ is more like a huge metropolitan city. There are different neighborhoods (like the photographers' neighborhood or the writers' neighborhood, the techy neighborhood). Sure, you can be connected with the people you know, but the real joy comes from taking walks through the city and finding interesting people that you don't know.

I can't think of a better way to sum up Google+. So in true social networking style, I've just shared his post with you here.

Social media enables you to find and chat with hundreds of thousands of people from around the world who share your interests, ideas, and beliefs. And you can agree with each other all day long. I think it's important to take time to add people to your Circles who have views that you wildly disagree with (or at least grumble about).

Google+ enables you to find a myriad of different people from all over the globe and all walks of life. Take time to discover people who aren't like you. They make the world (and your social network) much more interesting.

CHAPTER ONE

WHAT IS GOOGLE+ AND WHY SHOULD I USE IT?

In this chapter:

- + Discovering Why Google+ Is So Great
- + What Is the Difference between Google+ and Other Social Networks?
- + Does It Cost Money to Use Google+?
- + What Can You Do with Google+?
- + Who Can You Find on Google+?
- + Signing Up for Google+

G oogle is far more than just a search engine. The company has created a dazzling array of apps and services all aimed toward making the Internet a finer place to hang out: from its famous Maps, News, and Groups to its Google Earth projects, Google's gone out of its way to create really useful and fun Internet tools.

And recently Google added another tool to its toolbox: Google+. This is a cool take on social networking that takes some of the best components of other services and mixes in innovative features that make Google+ more useful, fun, and powerful. With more than 62 million users in the first six months, Google+ is off to a flying start. It's definitely time to sign up.

Discovering Why Google+ Is So Great

Unless you've been living on a technology-free desert island for the last 15 years, you've almost certainly heard about Google.

The famously playful company created the world's first truly useful search engine, cataloging and ranking the web (now over a trillion pages). Chances are that whenever you want to find something online, you Google it.

People are migrating to Google+ from other social networking services, such as Facebook and Twitter, or at least integrating it with their other social networking sites. While Facebook still has the edge in raw numbers (over 800 million active users), Google+ is getting bigger by the day. Unofficial Google+ statistician Paul Allen has predicted Google+ will have over 400 million users by the end of 2012.

Google+ offers so many advantages over other social networking services that it's hard to sum them up (although I cover them all throughout the book). It offers a refreshing change from other social networking sites with its range of new features, such as Circles, Hangouts, and Ripples, alongside integration with other Google services. It's also an amazing way to hook up and chat with groups of friends.

If you haven't signed up for Google+ yet, it's time to check out this new service. In this book I take you through all the features so you can make the most of this popular social networking site.

What Is the Difference between Google+ and Other Social Networks?

Chances are that you're already using Facebook and probably Twitter as well. Most social networking–savvy people are also integrating FourSquare, LinkedIn, Delicious, Reddit, and a fairly vast array of other social networking services into their lives.

So why would you want another social service? Well, for starters, Google+ has so many cool features you'd be crazy not to check it out. And even though it's similar to Facebook in many ways (see Figure 1-1), Google+ is already proving to be far more capable than Facebook when it comes to reaching the right people and more powerful than Twitter for keeping up with breaking news.

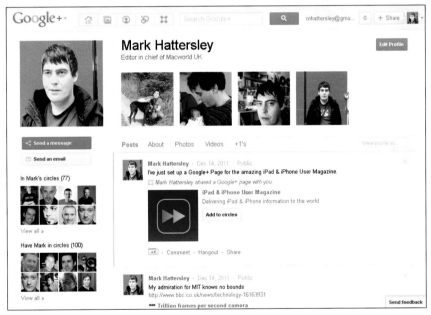

FIGURE 1-1 Google+ will look familiar to anybody who's used Facebook.

One of the really neat things about Google+ is the feature Circles, which enables you to organize your friends into handy groups: the defaults are Friends, Family, Acquaintances, and Following. It's also possible to create your own groups, such as one for a local club. You can then choose to share information with specific Circles of people or share it publicly with everybody. You can learn more about setting up and managing Circles in Chapter 5.

Google is on to something with Circles. Facebook considers all friends to be equal, whereas most human relationships are a bit more complicated. Since my nieces and nephews (not to mention my grandma) joined Facebook, I've had to be pretty careful about the sort of things I post. With Circles I can let loose with my friends, but keep it pretty clean-cut for the family.

Another really great feature with Google+ is public sharing and following. As on Twitter, on Google+ you can choose to follow people you don't know personally and see the things they share publicly. Like Twitter, Google+ doesn't require you to get approval to follow a person's public feed, so it's a great way to integrate your personal life with those of famous people you may want to keep tabs on.

Does It Cost Money to Use Google+?

The great thing about Google+ is that you don't need to pay to use the service. Some applications, notably Games, are free to use but may charge money for special features. It's possible (and indeed likely) that Google will introduce some form of advertising rates for businesses and users looking to gain extra exposure, but for most individuals, using Google+ is completely free and is likely to remain so permanently.

What Can You Do with Google+?

Like other social networking services, Google+ is all about sharing information. Using Google+, you can keep friends updated on what you're up to in life, where you are currently, and what your plans are.

It also provides a handy place to store an online profile, which can contain information on your occupation, employer, education, and where you've lived. While some people might balk at putting this information online, it's a great way to let potential clients and future employers know who you are, what you can do, and how to get in touch with you.

Who Can You Find on Google+?

With over 62 million members (and counting) Google+ is off to a good start, and chances are that you'll find most of your friends and work colleagues already on Google+. It helps that Google has spent many years building a collection of successful services that require a Google account, which people can use to sign up for Google+ immediately. Facebook is still ahead in the numbers game, so you'll probably find some friends and family members (especially the ones who aren't as technically forward as you) may not have signed up for Google+ yet.

Google also makes it easy to search through your contacts and find them (or invite them) to hook up with you on Google+. You can search for people you know using the built-in search engine, and Google+ uses people in your Circles (and the people who they know) to provide suggestions of people you might want to add to your Circles. It's also possible to use Yahoo! and Windows Live Messenger accounts to search through your contacts or upload your address book to add people you know into your Circles. Chapter 4 explains how to use Yahoo! and Windows Live Messenger with Google+.

Signing Up for Google+

One of the great things about Google+ is that it integrates with other Google services so neatly. And the odds are pretty good that you already have a Google account login and password. If you've ever signed up for Gmail, Google Maps, Google Earth, or most of the other Google services, then you already have a Google account, and that's your entry pass.

You don't need an invitation to join Google+, but you can still invite friends, as shown in Figure 1-2, and it's a good way to spread word of mouth.

FIGURE 1-2 Once you sign up for Google+, you are able to invite other users to take part.

GETTING A GOOGLE ACCOUNT

If you don't have a Google account, now is a great time to sign up for one. Getting a Google account is pretty easy: Go to www.google.com and click the Sign in button on the gray horizontal strip, known as the Google+ bar. (This strip appears whenever you are on any Google site; Chapter 3 has more information on using the Google+ bar). Click Sign up for a new Google Account to access the account creation page (see Figure 1-3).

FIGURE 1-3 Use this screen to create a Google account.

From here, you have to type information into the following text boxes:

+ **Your name.** Type your real name into the First and Last text boxes.

+ **Choose your username.** Type your desired username into the @gmail. com text box. This is your new Gmail email address, which you will use to sign in to Google+ and other Google services.

+ **Create a password.** Type a password that you use to access Google+ and other Google services. The password has to be a minimum of eight characters. An indicator to the right lets you know how strong the password is.

+ **Confirm your password.** Reenter the password to ensure that you have typed it in correctly.

+ **Birthday.** Use the Month, Day, and Year boxes to enter your date of birth.

+ **Gender.** Choose Male, Female, or Other from the drop-down list.

+ **Mobile phone.** Use the flag icon to choose your country, and then type your number into the Mobile phone text box. This is optional: you can still create an account without filling out this box.

+ **Prove you're not a robot.** Type the two words in the image into the Type the two pieces of text box.

+ **Location.** Use the drop-down list to choose your location.

+ **Privacy policy.** Select the I agree to the Google Terms of Service and Privacy Policy check box. By default, the check box to allow Google to use your account information to personalize +1's on content and ads on non-Google websites is selected. You can deselect this check box if you don't want Google to use your +1 information on non-Google websites.

- -

HOW DOES GOOGLE USE MY INFO WITH OTHER SITES? Google has a program called *AdSense* that displays Google ads on many different websites. Google uses the information about you from Google+ to personalize the kinds of ads you see on websites that use AdSense. It's up to you whether you want Google to do this (at least ads will be more relevant to you).

- -

Click Next step to go to the Create your profile page (see Figure 1-4). If you want to add a picture to your profile, click Add Profile Photo. Click Next step and then click Get started to complete your Google account.

FIGURE 1-4 You can add a profile photo on the Create your profile page.

After completing the sign-up procedure, you are taken to the default Google Search page, but the Google+ bar displays your name and provides access to Google+ and various Google account settings.

HOW DO I CHOOSE A GOOD PASSWORD? A really good way to create a strong but memorable password is to combine two different words with a + or & symbol between them, such as "fun&fair" or "telephone&call." Despite being easy to remember, these are surprisingly strong passwords and difficult for automated programs to hack.

VERIFYING YOUR GOOGLE ACCOUNT

Sometimes Google asks you to verify your account by entering your cell phone number (see Figure 1-5). Google then texts you (or an automated voice calls you) and provides a code. There are two options for getting the code:

+ **Text Message.** Google sends a text message containing the code to your cell phone. This is the default option, and I think it's the easiest because you get the code in written form.

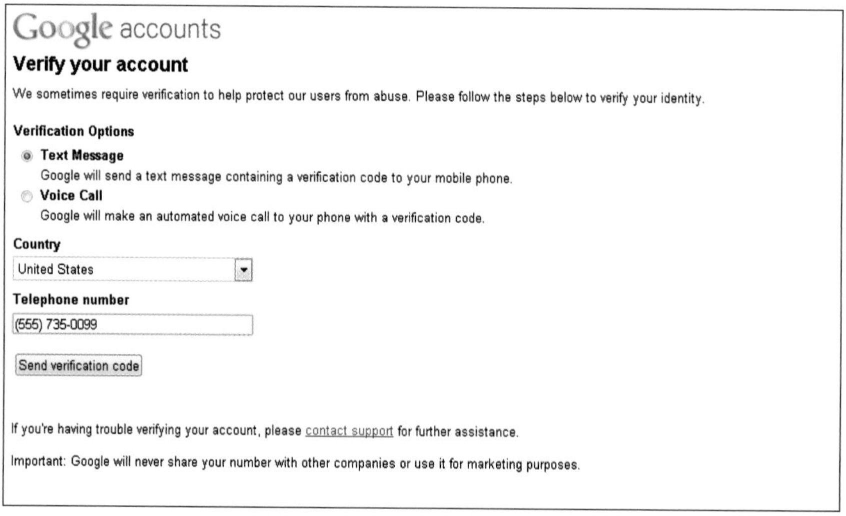

> Google accounts
>
> **Verify your account**
>
> We sometimes require verification to help protect our users from abuse. Please follow the steps below to verify your identity.
>
> **Verification Options**
> ○ **Text Message**
>   Google will send a text message containing a verification code to your mobile phone.
> ○ **Voice Call**
>   Google will make an automated voice call to your phone with a verification code.
>
> **Country**
> United States ▾
>
> **Telephone number**
> (555) 735-0099
>
> [Send verification code]
>
> If you're having trouble verifying your account, please contact support for further assistance.
>
> Important: Google will never share your number with other companies or use it for marketing purposes.

FIGURE 1-5 Google may ask you to confirm your details using an automated phone or a text service.

+ **Voice Call.** An automated voice service calls your cell phone and tells you the code. This is useful if you don't have a cell phone. You can write it down or type it directly into the text box on the web page.

Related Questions

+ How do I add information to my Google profile? **CHAPTER 2, Completing Your Google+ Profile**

+ How do I start using Google+? **CHAPTER 3, Navigating between Different Sections of Google+**

+ Should I worry about privacy with Google, and how do I manage my personal information? **CHAPTER 15, Discovering Just How Much Google Knows About You**

CHAPTER TWO

HOW DO I SET UP MY GOOGLE+ PROFILE?

In this chapter:

+ Signing In for the First Time
+ Completing Your Google+ Profile

After you activate your account, you need to set up your personal profile. This profile defines you publicly and is your chance to provide personal information and convey your personality. Your profile isn't just an exercise in vanity and self-promotion; it enables people to search for you and distinguishes you from other people who share your name.

Beyond giving people an idea of who you are and what you're interested in, your profile encourages them to add you to their Circles, initiate conversations with you, share items with you, and much more.

Signing In for the First Time

The first time you access Google+, you are asked to sign in with your Google account (as shown in Figure 2-1). Click Sign in, type your name and password, and click Sign in again.

FIGURE 2-1 Signing in to Google+ for the first time.

The first time you sign in to Google+, a series of pop-up displays asks you to add information to the service.

The first asks if you want to connect a Yahoo! or Hotmail account to Google+. Chapter 4 has more information on adding other services to a

Google+ account; for now, you can click Skip and Continue anyway to move on to Circle information.

Google+ recommends that you add at least ten people to your Circles before you start to use the service. You can use the search box to find people you know and add them to your Circles:

1. **Type the name of a person you know into the search box.** People matching that name appear in a list of results, as shown in Figure 2-2.

2. **Click Add to circles next to the correct person.** Four options appear in a drop-down list:

   + Friends

   + Family

   + Acquaintances

   + Following

3. **Choose an option from the list that best matches your real-life relationship with the person.** (*Following* is usually for people you don't know in real life but are interested in anyway, such as a celebrity.) A pop-up box appears describing Circles and how they work.

4. **Click Okay, got it.**

FIGURE 2-2 Finding people for your Circles for the first time.

When you have finished adding people to Circles, click Continue. You see a list of interesting and famous people that you can follow, as shown in Figure 2-3. Click Add next to groups of people you find interesting, and they are added to your Following Circle.

FIGURE 2-3 Adding groups of interesting people to the Following Circle.

Completing Your Google+ Profile

When you finish adding some basic information, you are taken into the Google+ website and can begin using the service. Before you start to use Google+ to find and communicate with people, you should complete your profile.

The basic information you added during sign-up (your name, your gender, birthdate and a photo) is enough to get started, but it's often better to add more information so people can get a better understanding of who you are.

Click the account icon (the profile photo thumbnail). The first time you click the account icon, a Welcome page appears that makes it easy to add several pieces of information to your profile, as shown in Figure 2-4.

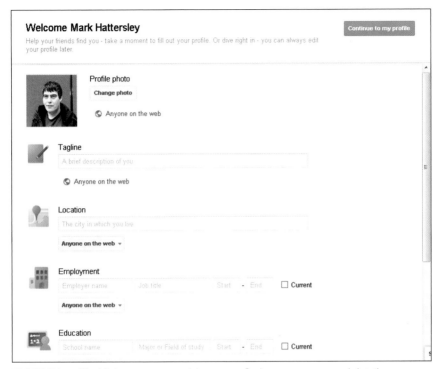

FIGURE 2-4 The Welcome page enables you to flesh out your personal details.

You can add information to these boxes:

+ **Tagline.** Type a short description of who you are. Mine says "Macworld UK Editor in Chief, book writer, all-round tech monkey."

+ **Location.** Enter the city in which you live.

+ **Employment.** You can add current and previous employment using the Employer name, Job title, Start, and End text boxes. As you fill out the boxes, another set appears underneath, enabling you to fill out more than one position. Select the Current box next to any jobs that you are presently working at.

+ **Education.** Add any history of your education using the School name, Major or Field of study, Start, and End boxes.

+ **Scrapbook.** Click Add Photo to add an image (or images) to your Scrapbook. This is a short collection of images (typically of you or things that relate to your life) that appears at the top of your profile.

Below some of the options is a drop-down list marked Anyone on the web. This means that anybody viewing your profile is able to see that information. You can also choose to share that part of your profile with just limited Circles (or even individual people). Click the Anyone on the web list and choose from the following options to limit visibility:

+ Anyone on the web

+ Extended circles

+ Your circles

+ Only you

+ Custom

Click Continue to my profile when you're done.

You'll be taken directly to the About section on the profile page (as shown in Figure 2-5). From here it's possible to fill out more detailed information. Click Edit Profile in the top-right to get the following options (you need to click on each part of the profile page to edit the information contained within it):

+ **A brief description of you.** This field is the same as the tagline you entered during sign-up. It's easy to overlook, as it's just below your name at the top of the screen. You can click on it to edit the brief description.

+ **Introduction.** This field enables you to add a further description of the things you do. In here, I've outlined all the different magazines and websites that I write for, the books that I've written, and some other personal information. You don't have to do this if you think the brief description is enough, although you can format the text here; for example, you can add bold, underline text, and create lists. You can also add links to web pages, so if you do a lot of different work on the Internet, this is a good place to promote it.

+ **Bragging rights.** You can use this field to outline any other achievements you're proud of. I have "Run the Brighton marathon" as one of my bragging rights.

At the bottom of the screen (below Occupation, Relationship, and the contact information boxes) are two other fields that you might want to note:

+ **Other names.** Here you can include any other names people might know you by. If you've changed your name or have a maiden name, then this is a good place to include it.

✛ **Nickname.** If you are known by any other name (nickname, alias, or simply a different name that you go by sometimes), then this is a place to put it. Remember that Google insists that the name you are commonly known as is used as your main name and that using any other name could lead to your account being suspended.

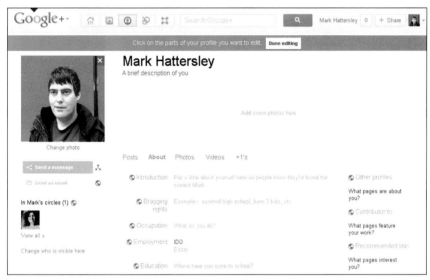

FIGURE 2-5 Editing the About part of the profile page.

That's an awful lot of personal information to be handing out online, so only put information on Google+ that you're comfortable having in the public domain. Take a look at Chapter 15 for more information on Google and privacy if you're concerned about having so much information online.

EDITING YOUR OCCUPATION, EMPLOYMENT, AND EDUCATION

Once your personal information is up to snuff, think about adding some professional data. This is particularly useful if you plan to use social networking on a professional level — you can use Google+ to promote yourself.

And you shouldn't underestimate the power of social networking (for both good and bad) when it comes to your career prospects. A survey by CareerBuilder.com in 2009 showed that 45 percent of all employers now check social media sites of prospective candidates during the hiring process.

So I think you should always include your occupational and educational information in Google+ and other sites, especially if you're proud of your achievements. The following fields are available:

+ **Occupation.** You can type a brief job title in this field and follow it with the company you work for. My occupation is listed as Editor in Chief at Macworld, IDG UK. You use a drop-down list to choose who can access this information: Anyone on the web, Extended circles, Your circles, Only you, or Custom (which enables you to choose specific Circles).

+ **Employment and Education.** Here you can fill out, or edit, your employment and education history. These fields may contain the information you entered when signing up for Google+.

You definitely need to be careful about what you post on social networking sites when looking for a job, but Google+ can be an incredibly powerful tool for conveying to employers your capabilities, personality, and positive attitude. Just be cautious.

WHAT SHOULD I DO WITH GOOGLE+ IF I'M JOB HUNTING?

Here's some good advice on using social networking if you're job hunting:

+ **Clean up your act.** The first thing you should do if you're looking for work is go through your current Google+ profile and remove any information that you think portrays you in a negative light.

+ **Be positive.** Make the effort to come across as a generally positive person to have in the workplace. Keep any gripes out of your social network.

+ **Check your Circles.** Make sure that you're only sharing personal information with the right Circles. Only friends and people you trust should be in your Friends Circle.

+ **Don't advertise your job hunt.** In general it's considered bad form to announce on a social networking site that you're looking for a new job while working for a company. Both current and prospective employers might not look too kindly on this kind of behavior.

MAPPING THE PLACES YOU'VE LIVED

Another really neat feature of Google+ is the way it uses Google Maps and Google's pretty extensive knowledge of world geography to map the places you've lived. If you've moved around a lot, this is a great way to keep in touch with people in the different areas where you've lived.

Rather than pinpointing locations on a map, just type the name of places you've lived into the Type a city name text box. When you type in the information, a new empty box appears beneath it so you can add more locations.

As with the other options, you can choose which Circles of people you share this information with.

Next to each location is a green pin; you can indicate your current location by clicking one of the pins. At that point the location moves to the top of the list and the pin next to it turns blue, as shown in Figure 2-6. Click Save when you're done.

HOW DO PEOPLE SEE MY MAP? When people view your About page in Google+, they see a map of the world with your locations on it as well as the list of places (as long as you've given them permission to view that part of your profile).

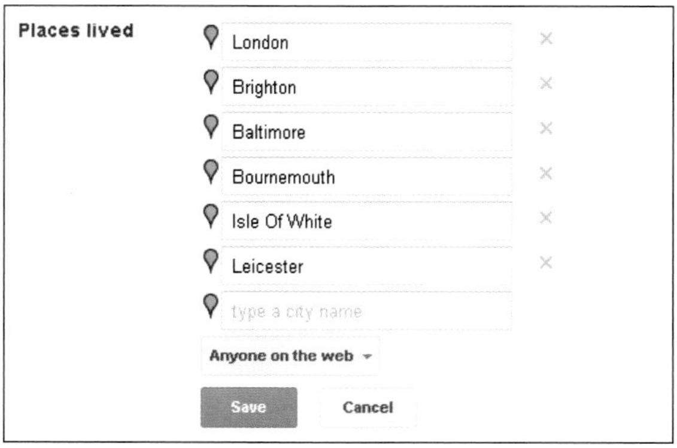

Places lived

- London
- Brighton
- Baltimore
- Bournemouth
- Isle Of White
- Leicester
- type a city name

Anyone on the web ⌄

Save Cancel

FIGURE 2-6 Use Google+ to create a map of all the places you've lived.

ADDING CONTACT INFORMATION

You should also consider adding your contact information on Google+. You can add a variety of information that enables people to get in touch with you, including the following:

+ Phone

+ Mobile

+ Email

+ Address

+ Fax

+ Pager

+ Chat

There are two sets of contact information fields, one for Home and one for Work, so you can add different details for both areas of your life. As you type information into each field, a new text field appears beneath it, enabling you to add multiple phone numbers, email addresses, and so on, for both Work and Home.

Don't feel you have to add all the information for each text field; you can pick and choose what information you want to enter and what you want to keep private. (I keep my cell phone number off social networking sites, for example.)

For each option you can also set which Circles of people can access each piece of information. If you're going to add personal contact information — especially your cell phone number — I generally advise you to pay close attention to Circles and make sure you're comfortable with the people you're sharing it with.

SETTING UP YOUR PERSONAL RELATIONSHIPS

It's also possible to set information about your current relationship using Google+. The following options are available:

+ I don't want to say

+ Single

+ In a relationship

+ Engaged

+ Married

+ It's complicated

+ In an open relationship

+ Widowed

+ In a domestic partnership

+ In a civil union

Oddly, at the moment you can't add the person you're in a relationship with, only that you're in a relationship, although I imagine Google will add this capability as time moves on.

You can also describe the sort of relationships you are interested in. Click the Looking for text field to bring up a set of four check boxes (as shown in Figure 2-7). You can select multiple relationships that you're interested in from the following list:

FIGURE 2-7 Listing the relationships you're interested in.

+ Friends

+ Dating

+ A relationship

+ Networking

As with other options, you can select which Circles are able to view this information. Click Save when you're done editing your Looking for status.

ADDING MORE PHOTOGRAPHS OF YOURSELF

One final thing on the About page is that you can edit the photo that you added during the sign-up procedure and add more photographs if you think one picture of you just isn't enough. Click the Add some photos here link to start adding photographs.

Click in the gray box marked Add Photo and choose the source of the photograph (in the same manner as when you added your profile picture). It's possible to add multiple pictures of yourself, as shown in Figure 2-8. They will appear below the brief description field.

Chapter 8 has more information on managing and uploading photographs to Google+.

FIGURE 2-8 It's possible to add multiple pictures of yourself to your About page.

Related Questions

+ What are Circles and how do I use them to manage which parts of my profile people can see? **CHAPTER 5, Getting to Know Circles**

+ How do I manage and upload images of myself using Google+? **CHAPTER 8, Uploading Photos and Creating Albums**

+ What is Google doing with my personal information? **CHAPTER 15, Discovering Just How Much Google Knows About You**

CHAPTER THREE

HOW DO I NAVIGATE GOOGLE+?

In this chapter:

+ Looking at the Google+ Home Page
+ Getting to Know the Google+ Bar
+ Navigating between Different Sections of Google+
+ Sending Feedback to Google

G oogle is famous for its clean, aesthetic design with minimal distractions. One look at the Google home page demonstrates this simplicity — it just shows a Google logo, a text box, and the two buttons Google Search and I'm Feeling Lucky.

Google can also be playful with its design, most often demonstrated in the famous Google Doodles. The Doodles replace the standard Google logo with a creative image to recognize a particular holiday, historical person, or event. (Clicking the Google Doodles logo links you to a website or Google Search result with more information on the origin of the design.)

But this playfulness never comes at the expense of users. Moreover, Google's design is the result of paying intense attention to users. On its philosophy page (www.google.com/about/corporate/company/tenthings.html), Google states the following:

> Since the beginning, we've focused on providing the best user experience possible. Whether we're designing a new Internet browser or a new tweak to the look of the home page, we take great care to ensure that they will ultimately serve *you*, rather than our own internal goal or bottom line.

And this is what Google says about its design philosophy:

> Above all, a well-designed Google product is useful in daily life. It doesn't try to impress users with its whizbang technology or visual style — though it might have both. It doesn't strong-arm people to use features they don't want — but it does provide a natural growth path for those who are interested. It doesn't intrude on people's lives — but it does open doors for users who want to explore the world's information, work more quickly and creatively, and share ideas with their friends or the world.

This pretty much sums up the Google+ interface as well. Like most Google websites, it has a beautiful Spartan design yet still provides easy access to a wide range of features. Indeed, the more you get to know the Google+ interface, the more you will get out of the service.

Looking at the Google+ Home Page

When you look at the Google+ home page, you can see that it's more feature-packed than the main Google page but still has the simplicity (a white background with clearly defined areas) that marks most Google designs. Figure 3-1 shows the different parts of the Google+ home page.

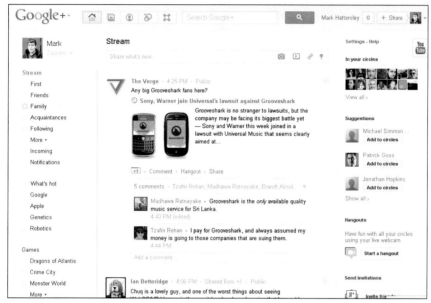

FIGURE 3-1 The Google+ home page.

The Google+ home page consists of four main elements:

+ **Google+ bar.** This gray strip sits at the top of the Google+ home page (and many other Google pages) and enables you to navigate Google services, search Google+, receive notifications, share posts, and access profile and account settings.

+ **Left-hand column.** This area contains your profile photo and a link to your profile. Beneath it you can access different areas of your Stream (covered next), What's hot, Games, and Chat. Chapter 7 has more information on chatting in Google+, and Chapter 9 has more information on What's hot and searching for news in Google+.

+ **Stream.** In the middle of the screen is the main display area with content that people have shared with you as well as your own recent posts.

+ **Right-hand column.** This area on the home page is typically used to provide suggestions to expand your use of Google+. It provides access to the following:

+ **Settings.** Click here to access the Google+ settings. Chapter 12 has more information on using Google+ settings.

+ **Help.** Click here to access the Google+ Support page (http://support.google.com/plus).

+ **YouTube search.** Click the YouTube icon to reveal a YouTube search box. Enter a search term and click the blue play icon. Google+ opens a pop-up window with a playlist relating to that search.

+ **In your circles.** This displays a series of profile photos of people from your Circles. Clicking on an image takes you to that particular profile, whereas clicking View all takes you to the Circles area of Google+.

+ **Suggestions.** People you might know are listed here. Click Add to circles and choose a Circle from the list to quickly populate your Circles with more people.

+ **Hangouts.** This enables you to start chatting with people using Google+'s Hangout feature. Chapter 7 has more information on Hangouts.

+ **Send invitations.** Though users do not need an invitation to join Google+, you can still click this link to send an email to people inviting them to join.

+ **Google+ Pages.** Click this link to set up a Google+ Page relating to a business, brand, service, or group that you might want to post about. Chapter 16 has more information on Google+ Pages.

+ **Games.** This displays icons of popular games that you can play in Google+. Chapter 11 has more information on gaming in Google+.

As you navigate different areas of Google+, the contents of the main display area change to reflect the options available in a given part of the service.

Getting to Know the Google+ Bar

In late 2011, Google introduced the Google+ bar. This gray bar (as shown in Figure 3-2) is at the top of all Google pages. If you are signed in to an active Google account, the contents of the bar change depending on the Google service you are using. On Google+, it displays the following:

+ **Google+.** Click on the Google+ logo (just the Google logo on other sites) to quickly navigate between different Google services.

+ **Navigation icons.** Five icons enable you to navigate the main sections of Google+: Home, Photos, Profile, Circles, and Games.

+ **Search Google+.** Typing a term into this text box searches for people and pages matching the search term.

+ **Account.** Click your name or account icon to access settings relating to your profile, account, and privacy.

+ **Notifications.** This small gray box changes to red if you have new notifications (described next). Click it to reveal what the activity is. If there is no new activity, it displays a 0.

+ **Share.** Click this icon to quickly share a post on Google+.

FIGURE 3-2 The Google+ bar.

NOTIFICATIONS

The small gray Notifications box turns red when you have notifications (alerts that Google wants you to know about). These can be from people who've added you to their Circles or people you've added who have added you back. Other notifications include people commenting on your post, accepting invitations, or clicking +1.

Notifications appear in a drop-down box that appears over the main web page, as shown in Figure 3-3.

You can use the Google+ Notifications box to do much more than you can with most notification boxes. Clicking on any notification of recent posts (either a post somebody has shared with you or one of yours where somebody has commented or +1'd) brings up a new display that shows the original post and any comments, as shown in Figure 3-4. From here you can add another comment to the post, +1 any post or comment, or mute the post. Clicking View all activity on my posts displays your Stream with all posts that have been reshared or commented on.

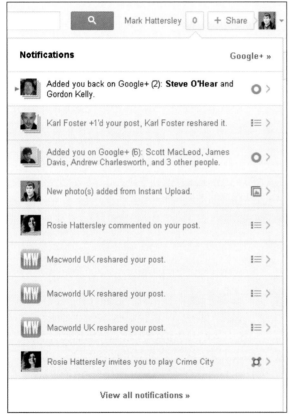

FIGURE 3-3 Google+ bar notifications.

It is also possible to manage your Circles directly from the Google+ bar by clicking Added you or Added you back in the list of notifications. A list of people who've added you to their Circles appears in the Notifications box and clicking Add to circles displays a drop-down list with your Circles to choose from.

FIGURE 3-4 Interacting with a notification in Google+.

SHARE

When you click the Share icon on the Google+ bar, a text box appears that enables you to create a new post for your Stream and share content directly from the bar, as shown in Figure 3-5. The most basic process is to simply type a message and click Share. By default the message is shared with the Public Stream, although you can share it with specific Circles by removing the Public icon (click the X on the green box). You can then add specific groups of people by clicking Add more people and choosing a group from the drop-down list.

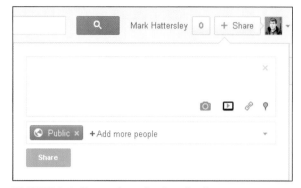

FIGURE 3-5 Sharing from the Google+ bar.

The Share section of the Google+ bar packs a lot of functionality into a small space. From left to right, the four icons in the lower-right of the text box enable you to share photos from your desktop or mobile phone; share videos from your desktop, YouTube, or phone; add links; and even add location data.

SHOULD I BE CAREFUL WHEN SHARING? Sometimes when you click Share, a dialog box pops up with a message: This post was originally shared with a limited audience — remember to be thoughtful about who you share it with. This means that the original post was only shared with a Circle that you are a part of, and is not public. So think carefully before clicking the Okay, got it! button.

PROFILE

Clicking either your name or your account icon in the Google+ bar brings up some links to various aspects of your profile. Unlike Notifications and Share, this part of the Google+ bar has limited options. Just four links are available:

+ Profile
+ Google+
+ Account settings
+ Privacy

You can also sign out of your account or switch accounts using the two links at the bottom of the profile box. Clicking Switch account switches to a separate menu (as shown in Figure 3-6). Clicking Sign in to another account enables you to log in with a second user account, which is handy if you share your computer with other members of the family. Both accounts will be logged in and appear as options when you click Switch Account.

FIGURE 3-6 Signing out and switching accounts using the Google+ bar.

Navigating between Different Sections of Google+

There are currently five main areas of Google+: Home, Photos, Profile, Circles, and Games, as shown in Figure 3-7. There are many ways to access the different areas, but typically you'll use the five icons to the right of the Google+ icon.

Clicking any of these icons changes the contents of the page, enabling you to work with a particular area of Google+. Although there's more to Google+ than these five areas, you spend most of your time working with them.

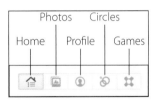

FIGURE 3-7 The navigation icons.

LOOKING AT YOUR STREAM

The default view of the home page shows the activity among the people within your Circles. Scrolling down the Stream reveals more stories listed in chronological order, and Google+ loads older stories as you continue to scroll.

If you haven't set up any Circles yet, you see a message in the Stream saying Not enough posts in your stream? (as shown in Figure 3-8). When you add people to your Circles, you see a photo slide show of new people who are sharing content with you (those who have added you to their Circles) and you can scroll down a list of recent activity from people you've added in your Circles, as shown in Figure 3-9.

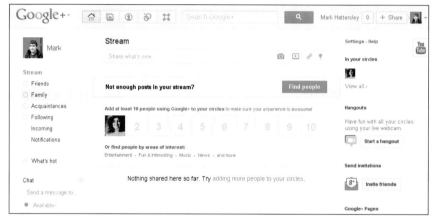

FIGURE 3-8 The Stream if you don't have enough posts in it.

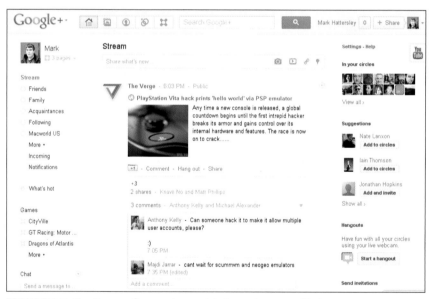

FIGURE 3-9 The Stream after you have added people to your Circles.

As you scroll down the page you can view the posts, including web links and photos, in your Stream. There are three main ways that you can interact with these posts:

+ **+1.** Clicking the +1 button indicates that you like the post. This activity will not appear in your Stream but other people viewing the post can see who has +1'd the post.

+ **Comment.** Clicking Comment brings up a text box that enables you to add your thoughts to the post.

+ **Share.** Clicking Share brings up a box (as shown in Figure 3-10) that enables you to type some text and add the original post to your Stream where it can be seen by people who are following you.

This covers the basics of interaction in the Stream. Chapter 6 has detailed information on how to share posts and manage other people's comments in your Stream.

FIGURE 3-10 Sharing a post in the Stream.

VIEWING PHOTOS

The second navigation icon enables you to view photos that people in your Circles have recently added. These appear in a montage in the main display area, as shown in Figure 3-11. When you hover the mouse over each picture, it expands slightly so you can get a closer look, and clicking on a photo displays it in a main window with a dark background so you can examine it closer. You can also interact with photos from this display, which is outlined in Chapter 8.

The right-hand column displays two groups of thumbnail photos: From your phone and Your albums. The left-hand column enables you to narrow down the types of photos being displayed using one of five options:

+ **Photos from your circles.** This is the default option and displays all photos from people who are in your Circles.

+ **Photos from your phone.** This displays all photos that you have uploaded using a mobile device. Chapter 13 covers using Google+ with a mobile device.

+ **Photos of you.** Choosing this option displays photos that people have tagged you in (indicating that the photo includes you).

+ **Photos from your posts.** This displays photos that you have posted on Google+.

+ **Your albums.** If you have arranged your photos into albums, this option displays all the photos in your albums.

You can also add new photos to Google+ by clicking the red Upload New Photos button on the right-hand side of the screen.

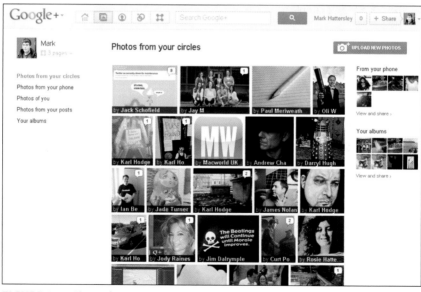

FIGURE 3-11 Photos from your Circles.

CHECKING YOUR PROFILE

Clicking the third navigation icon, profile, takes you to your profile page, as shown in Figure 3-12. (Setting up your profile is outlined in Chapter 2.)

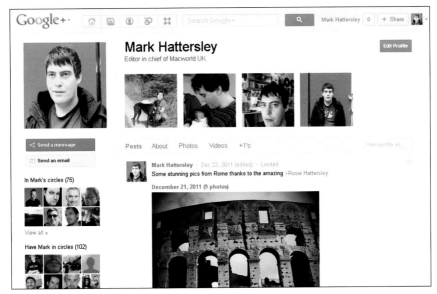

FIGURE 3-12 An example profile page.

The left-hand column displays your profile picture and thumbnail photos of eight people in your Circles and eight other people who have you in their Circles.

Clicking the Change who is visible here link below the Circles thumbnails enables you to adjust the contents of the left-hand column according to the following options:

+ **Show people in.** The left-hand column displays people in your default Circles: Friends, Family, Acquaintances and Following. Use the four circles drop-down list to turn these groups on and off, or you can change it to All circles. Deselecting the Show people in check box turns off this feature.

+ **Who can see this?** Two options are available here: Anyone on the web and Your circles.

+ **Show people who have added you to their circles.** Deselecting this check box hides the thumbnails of people who have recently added you to their circles.

Click Save if you're happy with the changes.

In the Stream you can see a row containing images of you (either ones you have added or ones other people have tagged as you) and the rest of the window contains a list of your posts. You can change the contents of the Stream using the five options below the images:

+ Posts

+ About

+ Photos

+ Videos

+ +1's

Clicking these options enables you to view the various parts of your profile.

VIEWING YOUR PROFILE AS ANOTHER PERSON Use the View profile as text box to see what your profile looks like to other people. You can type in the name of a person in your Circles, or click Anyone on the web.

TAKING A QUICK LOOK AT CIRCLES

Clicking the Circles icon displays a visual overview of all the people in your Circles, as shown in Figure 3-13. There's no left- or right-hand column in this view and instead the Stream displays a list of people Google+ determines relevant to you. You have three options for sorting the people shown, based on their relationship to you:

+ People in your circles

+ People who've added you

+ Find people

You can change the sort order from the default Relevance to First name, Last name, or Recently updated using the Sort by drop-down list.

You can drag the people displayed in the Stream to the Circle icons in the lower half of the window. Clicking a Circle changes the display to show the people in that particular Circle, and you can create new Circles here of your own choosing.

Chapter 4 outlines how to find friends and Chapter 5 explains how to manage your Circles.

FIGURE 3-13 Looking at people in your Circles.

SELECTING PEOPLE IN CIRCLES You can select multiple people from
the main display area in the Circles view by clicking on them or by dragging
a selection box around them.

ACCESSING THE GAMES STREAM

The final icon in the list enables you to play games directly within Google+.
Clicking the games icon displays games in the Stream, as shown in Figure 3-14.

A slide show of featured games is displayed in the Stream, and clicking Play
in the bottom-left of the image enables you to start playing the game. Games
launch and are played inside the Google+ website in your browser.

If any of your friends have played games, you will see their profile pictures
next to the Play button. The slide show moves pretty quickly, but you can
select a game from the list using the row of icons in the bottom-right of the
Stream.

The left-hand column has links to All games and Game notifications (typically notifications are for when you are playing a game with other people and it is your turn). It also displays a list of games that you have played recently.

FIGURE 3-14 The Games Stream.

NEW FEATURES Google is adding new features to Google+ all the time, so keep an eye on the navigation icons in case any new features are added.

Sending Feedback to Google

Another thing you can do from almost anywhere in Google+ is send feedback to Google about something on the site. Feedback is typically sent to report problems or errors, and providing this information can help make Google+ a better experience for anyone.

To send feedback, you click the Send feedback tab in the bottom-right of the screen. This displays a text box that enables you to describe the problem.

In some browsers (Google Chrome and Apple Safari), you can also highlight parts of the screen by drawing square boxes around areas of interest. Clicking Black out (shown in Figure 3-15) enables you to draw black boxes on the screen (which can be useful for removing any personal information that you don't wish Google's engineers to see). To remove the Highlight and Black out boxes, hover your mouse over them and click the X icons.

When you're happy, click the Preview button. This opens a new page (see Figure 3-16), which enables you to edit the description of the problem as well as view the additional information that is being sent to Google. Click the + symbols in the Additional information box to see what data is being sent. It also gives you a chance to double-check the screenshot that is being sent (although you cannot edit the image at this point).

If you're happy with what you want to send, click the Send feedback to Google button to send the comments on their way.

If you're using Microsoft Explorer, you will be presented with a text box enabling you to outline the problem. Type in your problem with the Google+ website and click Send feedback to Google. You will not see the Preview page.

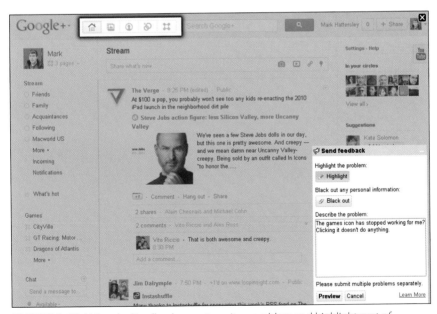

FIGURE 3-15 Using the Feedback page to write a problem and highlight part of the screen.

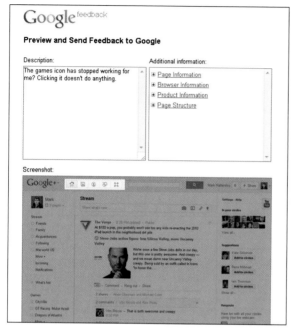

FIGURE 3-16 The Preview and Send Feedback to Google page.

Related Questions

+ My Circles are empty; how do I add people to them? **CHAPTER 5, Adding People to Circles**

+ How do I play games with people in my Circles? **CHAPTER 11, Installing Games**

HOW DO I FIND AND ADD FRIENDS?

In this chapter:

+ Searching for People You Know
+ Finding Friends from Your Contacts
+ Checking Out People Who've Added You

What use is a social network without friends? Without people to share with, you won't get a thing out of Google+, so as soon as you set up an account and password, you should find your friends.

Unlike Facebook, which intrinsically considers the relationships between you and your friends to be personal (with people you know in the real world), Google+ enables you to form relationships with people you haven't met in person by following their public posts. Often you find new people when your friends reshare people's posts. You can follow their posts, status updates, and other information they decide to share with you. In this sense, *friend* probably isn't the right word for everyone you interact with on Google+, which is why Google refers to friends as the more general *People in your circles*.

But that doesn't mean that all the people you follow on Google+ aren't your friends, and you're most likely to start with the people you know. In this chapter I show you how you can find your actual friends on Google+.

Searching for People You Know

The first step when adding people to your Circles is to look for people you know and see if they're already on Google+. Search is the one thing Google does better than any other company in the world, and because so many people have a Google account and use Google services in some form or another, your chances of finding the right person are pretty high.

You can search not only the information in people's profiles but also the information in Google+ posts, Sparks (snippets of news from around the web), and Hangouts. All this makes Google+ a pretty powerful way to find people you know.

To get started, type the name of somebody you know into the Search Google+ text box. The results of Google's search appear in a box below the search box, as shown in Figure 4-1.

The search results are split into two halves, with the top part displaying a list of relevant people. The number of people you see varies depending on the search term. If you search for somebody already in your Circles, that person appears at the top of the list. Chapter 5 has more information on Circles.

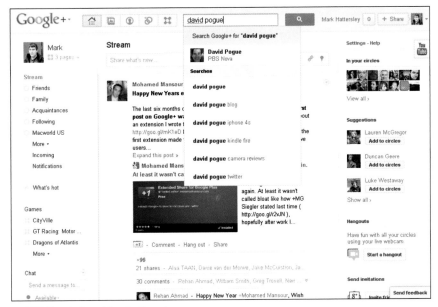

FIGURE 4-1 Searching in Google+.

Any Google+ Pages that relate to the person you've searched for appear below the list of Google+ profiles. Typically this occurs when you're searching for a celebrity who has fan pages as well as a Google+ profile. If no Google+ Pages are available, you see a list of related searches instead. Choosing one of these (or clicking Search Google+ for *search term*) brings up the search result inside the Google+ interface (as shown in Figure 4-2).

The search results page displays a larger image of the most likely profile result in the Stream, followed by posts containing the search result term. You can adjust the search with a number of different options on this page. The first drop-down list (marked *Everything* by default) enables you to narrow down the type of content you're searching for:

+ **Everything.** Click this link to display profiles, Sparks, and posts in the Stream.

+ **People and pages.** Click this link to display a list of names that match the search term and also the search term as it appears in posts and in users' profiles.

+ **Google+ posts.** Click this link to narrow the search to just display posts that contain the search term.

+ **Sparks.** Click this link to display Sparks (news stories) from the web that contain the search term. Sparks are outlined in more detail in Chapter 9.

+ **Hangouts.** Click this link to search through the people and typed messages used in Hangouts.

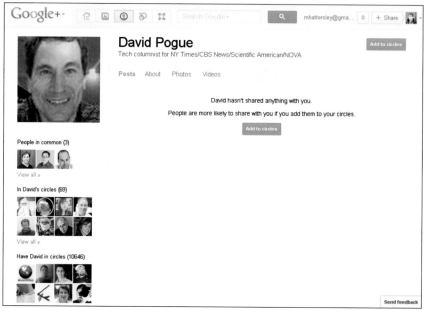

FIGURE 4-2 A Google+ search result.

The second drop-down list (set to *From everyone* by default) enables you to narrow down the search:

+ **From everyone.** Click this to get results from everybody on Google+.

+ **From your Circles.** Click this to get results from people added to your Circles.

+ **From you.** Click this to get results from your own posts.

The third drop-down list is set to *From everywhere* by default. This list enables you to narrow down searches to specific locations. Click the From everywhere link to reveal a text box. Enter the name of a location (either a city like San Francisco or country like France) to see posts from people in that part of the world.

The Stream also provides two options for displaying search results: Best of and Most recent. The way Google calculates the best results is something of a mystery, but I imagine it's a combination of the number of people following the poster and how many +1's the post has received. This is the default search results display. Clicking Most recent displays results in chronological order.

If you find yourself using the same search term over and over again (for example, if you like reading posts on a favorite subject such as robotics or gaming), then you can save this search:

1. **Type the term into the search box.**

2. **Click the blue Search icon.**

3. **Click Save this search.**

This adds the search term to the left-hand column where you can quickly access it. Although you wouldn't probably use this for people, it's good for keeping track of your favorite subjects and news events. To remove searches from the left-hand column, hover the mouse over it and click the X icon that appears.

THREE GREAT SEARCH TIPS

Here are three tips you might want to consider when using the search function in Google+:

+ **Search by subject.** Type a subject like **technology, fashion,** or **football** into the search bar. This brings up some high-profile people who mention that topic a lot, as well as Pages dedicated to the subject. You can also search for Sparks and add them to the left-hand column.

+ **Use online directories.** Though it's great to search for people in Google+, a number of online directories make it easy to get some inspiration and find high-profile people, or people with specific interests. Try Find People on Plus (www.findpeopleonplus.com).

+ **Share your searches.** You can share searches with friends (or post them on Google+). Just cut and paste the URL and pass it on to friends. For example, if you search for monkeys, the URL will look like this: https://plus.google.com/s/monkeys.

Finding Friends from Your Contacts

To boost the number of people in your Circles, use your contacts to quickly automate the process of adding people. This can save you from spending time searching for friends manually, and it is a great way to fill up your Circles.

You can add contacts from Yahoo! or Hotmail, or you can upload the information from a file exported from a program that contains your contacts (such as Outlook or Address Book).

Click the Circles icon and then click Find people to start looking for friends. When you start, Google+ displays a message saying You don't have anyone in your circles . . . yet!, as shown in Figure 4-3. As you start to add people to your Circles, other people will show up in the Stream in the Find people window. Google uses the relationships between people in your Circles to suggest people you might already know. (If you know several people and they all have added the same person to their Circles, Google predicts that you are likely to know this person as well.)

The more people you add to your Circles (see Figure 4-4), the more accurate the Find people results become.

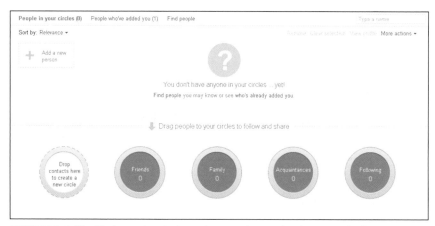

FIGURE 4-3 The Find people window when you have nobody in your Circles.

FIGURE 4-4 The Find people window when you have friends in your Circles.

ADDING CONTACTS FROM GMAIL You might be wondering about adding your Google contacts from Gmail. Weirdly enough, this isn't something Google+ supports, although it uses your connections to recommend people for you to follow. It is possible to export your Gmail contacts to a CSV file and import them (as you would with Outlook or Address Book).

FINDING FRIENDS FROM YOUR YAHOO! ACCOUNT

Aside from adding friends manually, you might want to import friends from your contact lists online. Google+ makes it easy to add people to Circles by including import functionality in the website.

Click the Circles icon, click Find people, and then click Yahoo!. A dialog box requesting sign-in details to Yahoo! appears, as shown in Figure 4-5. Follow these steps to connect your Yahoo! account to Google+:

1. **Type your ID into the Yahoo! ID text box.** This is normally your Yahoo! email address, such as mhattersley@yahoo.com.

2. **Type your Yahoo! password into the Password text box.** (Note that this isn't your Google+ password.)

3. **Verify that the Keep me signed in check box is unselected.** When this check box is selected, it ensures that you stay signed in to Yahoo!. You can keep it unselected because you're just going to use Yahoo! temporarily.

4. **Click Sign In.** You might have to type a CAPTCHA code (a graphic displaying letters that prevent automated computer programs from abusing the system).

5. **Click Continue.** The window displays a message saying you are authorizing access to Yahoo! contacts, profiles, and relationships.

6. **Click Agree.** Google+ can now access your Yahoo! information.

Google+ imports your contacts, and any contacts that are not already in your Circles appear in the Stream. You can drag the people to Circles to start following their Google+ posts.

FIGURE 4-5 Connecting Yahoo! to Google+.

IMPORTING CONTACTS FROM FACEBOOK TO GOOGLE+

Although it's not possible to import contacts directly from Facebook to Google+, it's possible to do so via Yahoo!. Follow these steps:

1. **Go to www.yahoo.com and sign in to your account (you may need to set one up if you don't have one).**

2. **Click Mail.**

3. **Click Contacts.**

4. **Click Import Contacts and choose Facebook.**

5. **Sign in to your Facebook account.** You will need to type your email address and password. Click Login.

6. **Click OK to enable Yahoo! to share your contacts.**

Now you just need to import your Yahoo! contacts into Google+ by following the instructions outlined earlier.

FINDING FRIENDS FROM WINDOWS LIVE MESSENGER

It is also possible to import contacts from a Windows Live Messenger account (also often referred to as Hotmail) into Google+ to add them to Circles. Follow these steps to connect Windows Live Messenger to Google+:

1. **Click the Circles icon, click Find people, and then click Hotmail.** A Connect Google to Messenger window opens, as shown in Figure 4-6.

2. **Type your Windows Live ID.**

3. **Type your password for Windows Live (not your Google+ password).**

4. **You can deselect the Connect automatically check box.** You only need to connect once.

5. **Click Connect.**

FIGURE 4-6 Connecting Google+ to Windows Live Messenger.

The people found in your Live Messenger contacts appear in the Stream of the Circles window. Drag them to your Circles to add them to Google+.

Checking Out People Who've Added You

Another great way to find people is to look for other people using Google+ who have added you to their Circles. Unlike Facebook, where you form one-to-one connections by accepting friends, in Google+ people can add you to their Circles independently (although they only get to read information that you post publicly). Chapter 6 provides more information on different types of posts.

To find people who've added you, click the Circles icon and then click People who've added you. The Stream displays a list of people who have added you to their Circles.

The Stream displays both people already in your Circles and those who you haven't added yet. You can tell which ones are already in your Circles because a small gray Circle icon appears to the lower-right of their names, as shown in Figure 4-7. People who aren't already in your Circles are displayed without the small gray Circle icon, and can be dragged to the blue Circles icons at the bottom of the screen.

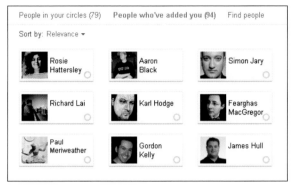

FIGURE 4-7 People who aren't already in your Circles do not have the gray Circle icon.

Another great way to discover the people you aren't already following but who have placed you in their Circles is to click Sort by and choose Not yet in circles from the drop-down list.

- -

ADDING FOLLOWERS You can quickly add all people following you by clicking More actions, clicking Select all, and then dragging the selections to the Following Circle.

- -

Once you have started to add people to your Circles, you can view posts from them in your Stream.

Related Questions

+ What are Circles and how do I manage them? **CHAPTER 5, Getting to Know Circles**

+ How do I remove people from Circles? **CHAPTER 5, Removing People from Circles**

+ How do I share information with people who are in my Circles? **CHAPTER 6, Choosing Which Circles to Share Your Posts With**

CHAPTER FIVE

WHAT ARE CIRCLES AND HOW DO I USE THEM?

In this chapter:

+ Getting to Know Circles
+ Adding People to Circles
+ Removing People from Circles
+ Creating New Circles
+ Editing and Sharing Circle Information
+ Blocking People

Google+ connections are different from friends on Facebook. Instead, you have *People in your circles*. Think of Circles as the groups of people you know. These groups are based on the different categories of social bonds — for example, three of the default Circles are Friends, Family, and Acquaintances. You can add and edit Circles to match the relationships you have in the world.

Unlike Facebook, where you make one-to-one connections, on Google+ you don't actually need to be friends with people or get their approval to have them in your Circles and follow their posts. The people you put into your Circles can be people you know or just like. They get notification that you're following them and they can block you if they choose, but otherwise you receive any posts they make publicly. In this sense, Google+ blends the best of open social networks like Twitter with closed ones like Facebook. But it all depends on getting your Circles right. In this chapter I show you how Circles work.

Getting to Know Circles

Personalizing your Circles makes for a much better Google+ experience. Because of this, you'll spend some time managing and adjusting your Circles to match the ebb and flow of your social groups and changing interests over time.

Start by clicking the Circles icon in the icon bar. This displays the Circles in the Stream, as shown in Figure 5-1.

At the top of the Stream you see all the people you have found and added to your Circles. The lower half of the Stream contains the default four Circles (displayed as blue circular graphics):

+ **Friends.** As the name suggests, these are people who you know intimately and share your life with.

+ **Family.** These are family members. You might want to share different information with family than friends, for example.

+ **Acquaintances.** These are typically work colleagues, although they can be anyone with whom you have a relationship but wouldn't want to share anything personal.

+ **Following.** These are people you are interested in but don't know on a personal level. People who post material publicly (as I do) share information with people following them.

FIGURE 5-1 The Circles in the Stream.

These are the four main Circles; however, it is possible to customize Circles to create a set of categories that work for you. You do this using the gray Drop here to create a circle icon to the left of the default Circles.

IN TWO CIRCLES You can add a person to more than one Circle. My two sisters Wendy and Vicky, for example, are in both my Friends and Family Circles.

Adding People to Circles

One of the great things about Google+ is just how interactive the web page is. Unlike Facebook, which largely involves clicking and selecting (like a regular web page), Google+ enables you to click and drag items.

A great example is adding people to your Circles. If you want to add a person from the Stream to a Circle, you click on a profile photo thumbnail and drag it over a blue Circle icon at the bottom. A green +1 graphic shows that the addition has been successful (if a person is already in the Circle, the photo thumbnail slides back up to the Stream).

It is also possible to add several people to Circles at once by clicking multiple people in the Stream. As you click them, they become highlighted in blue (as shown in Figure 5-2). Dragging them to a Circle adds all the selected people. You can deselect individual people by clicking each one a second time, and you can deselect all the selections by clicking Clear selection or by clicking in the white space between the people in the Stream.

FIGURE 5-2 Multiple selections in the Circles Stream.

You can also use the Selected link to view just the people highlighted in the Stream. This is useful if you're selecting a lot of people to add to a Circle and want to double-check you've chosen the ones you want without the clutter of unselected people.

- -

CIRCLE IDENTIFICATION As you hover the mouse above people in the Stream, the Circles that they are in light up with a blue glow.

- -

Removing People from Circles

Of course, you may want to remove people from Circles (say if a work colleague has left or if you simply no longer want to follow a person's updates).

Removing a person from a Circle is a straightforward process. The easiest way to do it is to drag the person from the Circle (as shown in Figure 5-3). Follow these steps:

1. Hover the mouse over a Circle to reveal the people contained within that Circle.

2. Click and hold the mouse over a person.

3. Drag him or her out of the Circle and let go.

A red trash icon appears to indicate that a person is being removed from a Circle. If you accidentally drag the wrong person from the Circle, it is possible to cancel the move by dragging the profile photo thumbnail back inside the Circle before releasing the mouse (or you can always search again and add that person to a Circle).

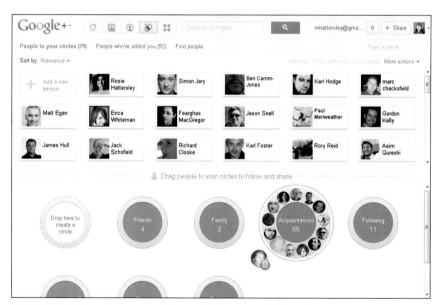

FIGURE 5-3 Dragging a person from a Circle removes him or her.

A more detailed method for removing people from a Circle is to move the Circle into the Stream to edit it. This is especially useful if you want to remove multiple people at once. Do the following:

1. **Click a blue Circle at the bottom of the screen, or click and drag the Circle from the lower half of the screen to the people on the top half of the screen.** The Stream displays people in that particular Circle (as shown in Figure 5-4).

2. **Click to select people in the Stream whom you want to remove.** You can select multiple people.

3. **Click Remove (near the top of the screen) to take them out of the Circle.**

4. **To return to the main display of all the people in your Circles, click People in your circles.**

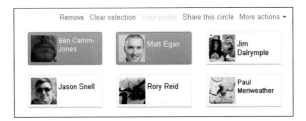

FIGURE 5-4 Use the Remove link to delete people from a Circle.

It is possible (although somewhat convoluted) to move a person from one Circle to another (for example, if a friend becomes a member of your family). To do this, click a Circle at the bottom to reveal the people in that Circle in the Stream. Then drag a profile photo thumbnail from the Stream to the desired Circle; this copies that person to that other Circle (but does not delete him or her from the original one). With the profile photo thumbnail still highlighted, click Remove to bounce that person from the Circle.

- -

EDITING MULTIPLE CIRCLES SIMULTANEOUSLY It's possible to select multiple people from different Circles and copy them all at once to a new Circle. If you have two people from Family and one from Acquaintances highlighted and drag the one person to Friends, all three are copied to the new Circle.

- -

COMPLEX CIRCLE NAVIGATION

Another neat trick to learn is how to perform detailed navigation of people within Circles. You can view the people in a Circle as well as drill down to selected people using the following steps:

1. **Click a Circle to view the people in the Stream.**

2. **Click and select people from the Circle (now displayed in the Stream).**

3. **Click Selected to view just the selected people in the Stream.**

4. **Click the Circle link above the Stream (for example: Family) or click a blue Circle icon at the bottom of the Stream to switch back to viewing all the people from that Circle.**

5. **Click People in your circles to move back to viewing all the people in the Stream.**

This technique is great to learn when your Circles become large and you want to narrow them down or split them into several smaller Circles.

Creating New Circles

The longer you use Google+, the larger your Circles may become; at this point you start to come across the limitations of having just the default four circles.

If you work for a large organization, you might consider splitting up Acquaintances into smaller Circles. I have Circles for the Macworld team, the wider Editorial team I work with, and everybody in the world I work with.

To create a new Circle, drag a group of highlighted people to the empty gray Circle. Here are the specific steps:

1. **Click multiple people in the Stream to select them.**

2. **Drag the selected people to the empty Circle that says Drop here to create a circle.** The people are added to the new Circle. You can also add other contacts from other Circles to the new Circle once it is created.

3. **Click Create Circle.** This brings up an edit box, as shown in Figure 5-5.

4. **Type a name for the Circle in the Circle name text box.**

5. **Add a description for the Circle by clicking the Click to add a description link.** This brings up a new text box and allows you to type a description up to 350 characters long. (This step is optional.)

6. **If you wish, continue adding people by clicking Add a new person.** However, I think it's better to use the Stream to place everyone in the Circle first.

7. **Click Create circle with X people (where X is the number of selected people) to add the new Circle to the Stream.** The new Circle appears at the end of the current list in the Stream.

It is possible to skip the first three steps in the preceding list and create a completely empty Circle by clicking Create circle in the empty gray Circle icon. This is useful if you want to create an empty Circle and populate it with people later.

FIGURE 5-5 Fill in this information to create a new Circle.

- -

ORDERING CIRCLES It's possible to reorder the Circles by clicking and dragging them into new positions.

- -

Editing and Sharing Circle Information

Another good technique to learn in Google+ is how to edit Circle information. This is handy if a Circle becomes larger than your original intention (my

Macworld Circle eventually became too broad to incorporate all the affiliated people I know, so I renamed the Circle Macworld US and created other Circles for Macworld UK, Macworld Spain, and so on).

To edit a Circle, click the Circle to open it in the Stream. Along with the people appearing in the Stream, the Circle now contains three links (as shown in Figure 5-6):

+ **Edit.** Clicking this opens a window where you can change the Name and Description of the Circle.

+ **Delete.** Clicking this removes the Circle. When a warning message appears, click Delete circle to confirm the deletion. The Circle rolls off to the right of the screen and an Undo link appears in a yellow box above the Google+ bar. This link remains until you move away from Circles and into another area of Google+, at which point you are not be able to recover the Circle.

+ **Share.** This option enables you to share the people in the Circle with people in other Circles (as shown in Figure 5-7). Share does not appear in an empty Circle.

FIGURE 5-6 Selected Circles display Edit, Delete, and Share links.

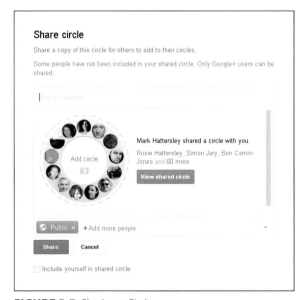

FIGURE 5-7 Sharing a Circle.

Follow these steps to share a Circle:

1. **Open a Circle and click Share.**

2. **Write a description of the Circle for the people in the other Circles to read.** Note that the Add circle link and View shared circle button do not do anything; they are just graphics displaying what is being shared.

3. **Click Add more people to choose which Circles or people to share the Circle with.** Click the X icon to remove Circles.

4. **You can choose to contact people who are in your Circles but not yet using Google+ by choosing the Also email *X* people not yet using Google+ check box (where *X* is the number of people).** This appears if there are people in your Circles not yet using Google+.

5. **You can include yourself in the shared Circle by selecting the Include yourself in shared circle check box.**

6. **Click Share.**

Sharing Circles is a great way to increase the profile of both yourself and your friends when you start creating custom Circles (such as work groups or friends with a shared hobby). You can even create Circles and share them with the Circle itself, so other people can use the same Circle you do.

- -

REWRITING THE PAST If you delete a Circle, it doesn't just prevent your future posts from appearing in the Stream of the former Circle members; it also removes anything in the past you have shared with them (unless you shared it via another Circle as well).

- -

Blocking People

Most of the time, if you no longer wish to hear from people, then removing them from your Circles is a perfectly good option.

Sometimes, unfortunately, you may end up with a person in a Circle who is overly rude, offensive, persistent, or just plain antisocial. It's never really happened to me on Google+, but these people are out there. And if you are unfortunate enough to come across one, you may decide that blocking that person is the best way forward.

Blocking people does the following things:

+ You no longer see their content in your Stream.

+ They aren't able to comment on your content.

+ They are removed from your Circles.

+ They are still able to see your public posts.

Blocking people, while not a pleasant task, is a good way to stop them from bothering you. Follow these steps to block a person from your Google+ account:

1. **Select the unwanted individual in the Circles area.**

2. **Click More actions, and in the drop-down list choose Block.** A warning message appears informing you that you will no longer be able to view that person's content, and that person won't be able to comment on your posts.

3. **Click Block *Name* (where *Name* is the person you're blocking) or Report and block this person.**

Choosing Report and block this person alerts Google to that individual's behavior. Typically Google doesn't get personally involved in bad behavior or personal squabbles, even if the behavior is harassing and upsetting you personally. But if the person is acting illegally (if you believe they are disturbing minors, for example) or if you believe they are trying to scam or extort you, then I'd advise you to click Report and block this person. If you do, Google+ brings up a further menu asking you to choose from the following options:

+ Spam

+ Nudity

+ Hate speech or violence

+ Child abuse

+ Copyright

+ Impersonation

+ Fake profile

+ Other

Choose the appropriate option and click Submit.

IN THE DARK People don't receive a message from Google saying that you have blocked them. However, if they check the People who've added you area of Google+, they may notice that you are no longer following them.

It is possible to unblock people if you change your mind later. To do so follow these steps:

1. **In the Circles area, click More actions, and in the drop-down list, choose View blocked.**

2. **A window appears displaying a list of blocked people (see Figure 5-8).**

3. **Click Unblock next to the person you want to appear again.** A message appears saying the person was unblocked. The person won't automatically return to the original Circle, though.

4. **If you want to add the person back to a Circle, click Add to circles and choose a Circle from the list.**

5. **Click Done.**

Blocking is something I do with caution. It is a fairly heavy-handed approach and is best suited for people who really are harassing you, rather than friends whom you've had a falling out with. If you are merely unhappy with a person, remove them from your Circles first.

Having said that, people removed from your Circles can still comment on your posts, so blocking them is a good way to prevent nuisance Google+ users from making unkind comments on your posts. See Chapter 6 for more information on managing your posts.

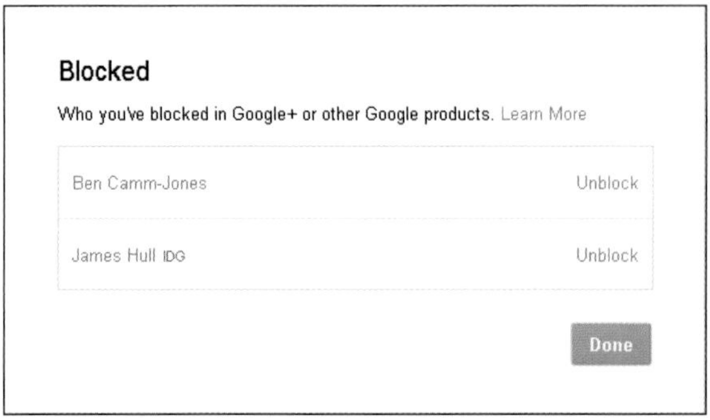

FIGURE 5-8 Unblocking people from Google+.

Related Questions

+ How do I add new people to Circles? **CHAPTER 4, Searching for People You Know**

+ How do I use Circles to share things with different groups of people? **CHAPTER 6, Choosing Which Circles to Share Your Posts With**

+ How do I stop people from commenting on my posts? **CHAPTER 6, Disabling Comments**

HOW CAN I SHARE WHAT'S HAPPENING IN MY LIFE?

F inding people and setting up Circles is a vital part of the Google+ experience. The other part is using Circles to share what's happening in your life. Sharing is the key ingredient of all social networking sites: the more you post, the better your experience will be.

A post can share anything from what you're doing right at that moment to something cool you've discovered. It can also just be your thoughts or opinions. Posts can be plain text or include links to websites, video clips, photos, and even your geographic location.

A cool thing about Google+ is that you can share posts with different Circles, which is what makes it a really powerful social media network. It also makes it a bit more complex to use than Facebook or Twitter but ultimately, much more rewarding. In this chapter I show you all the cool things you can do with your posts.

Creating a Post to Share in Your Stream

Posting a message from within Google+ is an unsurprisingly simple process (it'd be a bit strange if Google made it complicated). To quickly create a message and share it with the world, do the following:

1. **Click the home icon to make sure you're on the home page.**

2. **Type your message into the text box at the top of the Stream (as shown in Figure 6-1).**

3. **Click Share.**

FIGURE 6-1 A post in the Stream.

Your first post is shared publicly (with everybody who is following you or people who have you in their Circles). When you start to select different

Circles (I come to that in a bit), then the default posting option is the Circles you used in the last post.

You can cancel a post before sharing it by clicking the X icon in the top-right of the text box.

Writing plain text posts is a good way to quickly share what you're doing, but ultimately, you'll be a better Google+ user if you put a bit more effort into your posts. Here are some of the other things you can share:

+ **Photos.** You can add images from within Google+, from your smartphone, from the web, or from your desktop to Google+.

+ **Videos.** It's possible to upload videos from your computer or mobile phone, or share them from YouTube directly within Google+ (you can also cut and paste links from other video-sharing sites).

+ **Links.** You can add links to web pages that you've viewed in your posts.

+ **Location information.** It's also possible to add your current location.

You add all these items using the small icons to the bottom-right of the text box (see Figure 6-2). Adding mixed media to your posts makes them more creative and lets you share the things that are going on around you and on the wider web. A lot of people use Google+ almost like a blogging platform, creating long and detailed posts packed with images, video, and location information.

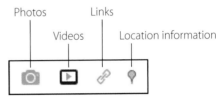

FIGURE 6-2 Click these icons to add photos, video, links, and location information.

FORMATTING TEXT IN A POST

One question that many people ask is whether they can format text in posts (make text bold, underline, and so on). Google+ doesn't have the usual text formatting icons that you find in many text editing programs, but you can add some basic formatting using the following formatting tips (as shown in Figure 6-3 and Figure 6-4):

+ Place text between asterisks *like this* to write in bold.

+ Place text between underscores _like this_ to write in italics.

+ Place text between hyphens -like this- to strikethrough text.

You can also place multiple symbols between the brackets for multiple effects. Using the *_ symbols makes text both bold and italicized.

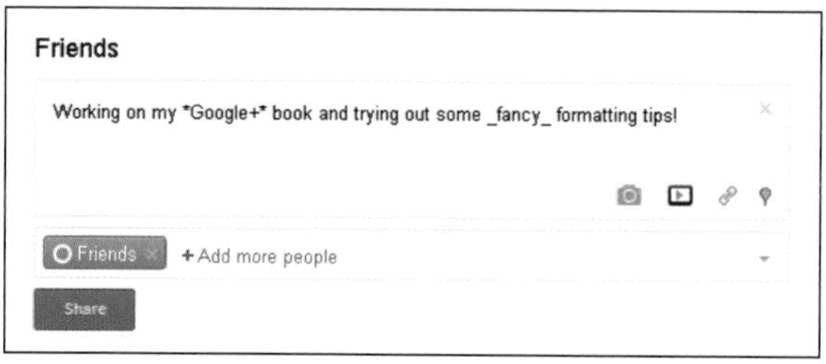

FIGURE 6-3 Formatting text in a Google+ post.

FIGURE 6-4 The formatted text.

ADDING IMAGES TO YOUR POSTS

One of the most obvious things you can add to a post is images — these can be found on other websites, stored within Google+, located on your computer, or taken on a mobile phone. Follow these steps to quickly add an image to your post:

1. **Click the green Add photos icon.**
2. **Choose Add photos from the drop-down list.**
3. **Choose photos from your computer using the Open window.**
4. **Click Open.**

The image or images appear below the text in your post (if you select multiple images they appear as a slide show, as shown in Figure 6-5). You can add additional images to the post by clicking Add more, and you can rotate and remove images by clicking Edit photos. Chapter 8 has more information on adding, editing, and managing photos in Google+.

FIGURE 6-5 Adding photos to posts.

DRAG AND DROP IMAGES In Google Chrome and Safari, you can add individual images to Google+ by clicking on and dragging the images from the Finder or desktop straight to the Google+ text box.

ADDING VIDEO CLIPS TO YOUR POSTS

The next step up from adding photos to your posts is adding video clips. It is similar to sharing photographs in that you upload the video from your desktop to Google+. However, it's more typical for people to use an online service like YouTube to share the video and then share that link within Google+.

To share a video in a post, click the Add video icon and choose one of the following options:

+ Upload video

+ YouTube

+ From your phone

The first two options require you to manually add video that is either stored on your computer (as shown in Figure 6-6) or already on Google's YouTube video service. The last option, uploading video from a mobile phone, is especially interesting (especially if you have a phone running Google's Android operating system) because it uploads all the video you take from the phone to an online storage area; you then pick and choose which videos to post to Google+.

FIGURE 6-6 Choosing a video file to upload.

Uploading a Video

To upload a video file to a post, follow these steps:

1. **Click the Add video icon and choose Upload video.**

2. **Click Select videos from your computer.** Alternatively, drag a file from Windows Explorer (or Finder on a Mac) to the Upload videos window.

3. **Use Windows Explorer (or Finder on a Mac) to locate the video file and click Open.** It takes a few moments for the video to upload to Google+ and be processed (formatted into a video format playable in Google+).

4. **Click Add videos.**

The video clip appears under your post (as shown in Figure 6-7). You can still add text to it and choose which Circles to share it with before clicking Share. To remove the video clip, click the small X icon to the right of the clip.

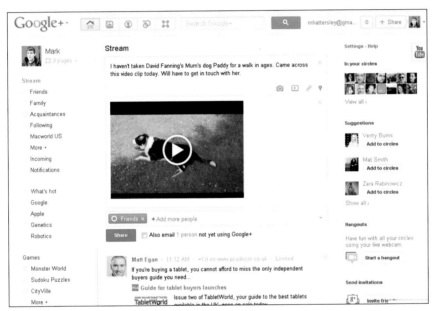

FIGURE 6-7 The video clip appears in the post.

Using YouTube

To add a video clip from YouTube to Google+, follow these steps:

1. **Click the Add video icon and choose YouTube.**

2. **You have three options for including a video (displayed in the top-left of the Choose a YouTube video window):**

+ **Search.** Type a search term into the text box. Choose a video from the search results and click Add video.

+ **Enter a URL.** If you have a URL for a YouTube video, type it into the text box and click Add video. Note that it has to be a YouTube URL, not just a video clip from a website.

+ **Your YouTube videos.** Any videos you have uploaded to YouTube appear in the window (as shown in Figure 6-8). Choose a video from the list and click Add video.

The video appears below your post. Edit your text and click Share to send the video out into the world. When you insert a YouTube video, a brief text description (taken from YouTube) appears below the video. It cannot be edited in Google+.

PASTING DIRECT LINKS It's also possible to post links to YouTube clips by copying and pasting the URL directly into the post. The URL will not appear as part of the post. This technique also works with some other video-sharing sites, such as Vimeo.

WHAT FILES CAN I UPLOAD?

Any video you capture using a modern digital camera or cell phone should be compatible with Google+. But if you're archiving old video footage, you may need to know what file formats to use. Here is a list of compatible file types:

+ WebM

+ MPEG-4

+ 3GPP

+ MOV

+ AVI

+ MPEG-PS

+ WMV

+ FLV

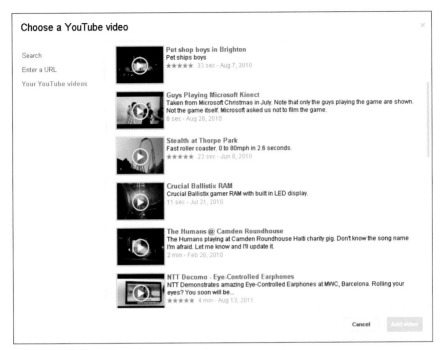

FIGURE 6-8 Choosing video from your YouTube account.

ADDING LINKS TO WEB CONTENT

One of the key parts of any social networking experience is sharing the information, articles, and entertaining content you find on the web with your friends.

Posting links to web content is incredibly easy in Google+. As you'd expect from a company that cut its teeth on making it easy for people to find content, Google has gone out of its way to help you share the stuff you find on the Internet. There are a number of different ways you can share links in Google+:

+ **Add link icon.** Click the Add link icon, cut and paste (or type) the link into the text box, and click Add.

+ **Cut and paste.** Simply cut a URL and paste it into your post.

+ **Google +1.** Many websites now display the +1 icon with interesting articles. You can click this to indicate that you like the page, but you can also write a comment and share it in Google+ from within the web page itself (as shown in Figure 6-9).

FIGURE 6-9 Sharing a link in Google+ from another website.

+ **Drag and drop.** You can drag a URL directly to the Google+ post using Google Chrome or Safari web browsers (but not Internet Explorer). First click in the Share text box to activate it. Then drag the URL icon (the small icon to the left of the URL — it appears as a world icon in Google Chrome) directly to the text box.

The link appears below your post with the headline, a sample of text, and an image from the website (as shown in Figure 6-10). You can use the left and right arrows to change the sample image, or click the X icon to remove the image.

FIGURE 6-10 The post as it appears in your Stream.

ADDING LOCATION INFORMATION

Another really neat thing you can add to your posts is location information, the specific place where you are posting at that moment. You might do this because you're at an event or show and want to tag it or because you're post-ing about that part of the world. I often do this whenever I'm talking about a cool tourist spot I'm visiting. That way people can pinpoint where I'm talking about as well as read my posts and see my photographs.

Location information works in Google Chrome, Safari, and Firefox but not in some browsers such as Internet Explorer.

HOW CAN GOOGLE TELL WHERE I AM? Google uses a mixture of IP (Internet protocol) addresses and triangulation of known cellular data tow-ers and known Wi-Fi networks (which it has mapped out while creating Google Street View). If your device has GPS, it also uses this for a reason-ably exact match. Google+ uses all these to determine your location.

Follow these steps to add your location information:

1. **Type in your post and click the Add your location icon.** The first time you add a location, your web browser brings up a message in the top of the bar saying Google+ wants to track your physical location, as shown in Figure 6-11.

2. **Click Allow.** The address you're at (or thereabouts) appears below the post, as in Figure 6-12.

3. **Click the address, which is a link to Google Maps.** You can see how accurate the location information is (it isn't possible to adjust it in Google Maps, though).

4. **Click Share.** The post appears with the address listed below the text. Other people can click the link to open Google Maps and view your location along with the post.

I typically don't recommend sharing your home location with people you don't know that well (although some people do it all the time with little con-cern). If you are cautious about location sharing, however, read Chapter 15 on managing your privacy and personal information.

https://plus.google.com wants to track your physical location
Allow
Deny

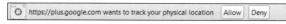

FIGURE 6-11 Click Allow to enable location sharing.

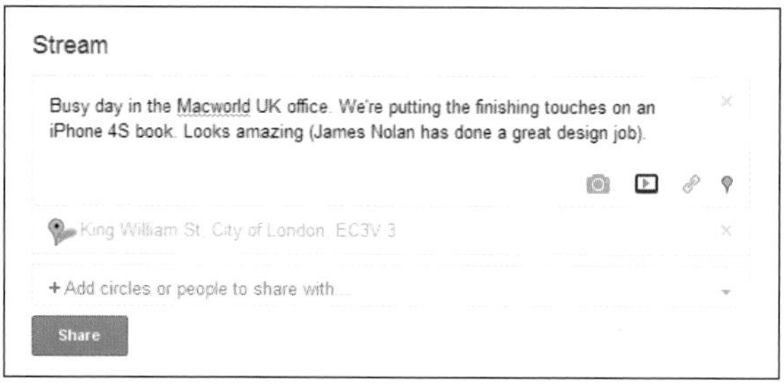
Stream
Busy day in the Macworld UK office. We're putting the finishing touches on an iPhone 4S book. Looks amazing (James Nolan has done a great design job).
King William St, City of London, EC3V 3
+ Add circles or people to share with...
Share

FIGURE 6-12 The location appears as a link below the post.

WHY WON'T GOOGLE+ SHARE MY LOCATION?

By default, web browsers do not normally allow web pages to access your location without your permission (for security reasons).

If you want to share location information, Google+ may present a warning message. If you receive this message, you need to follow these steps to share location information in the Google Chrome web browser:

1. **Click the wrench icon in the Google Chrome web browser (the icon on the far-right of the toolbar).**
2. **Choose Options on a PC (Preferences on a Mac) and click Under the Hood (or Under the Bonnet in some locations).**
3. **Click Content Settings.**
4. **Under Location, choose Allow all sites to track my physical location or Ask me when a site tries to track my physical location.** You use the third option, Do not allow any site to track my physical location, if you do not want to allow location sharing.
5. **Click the X icon in the top-right of the screen to close the settings.**

When you return to Google+, you should be able to share information about your location. I don't recommend allowing all websites to track your physical location.

Choosing Which Circles to Share Your Posts With

As you may have noticed, Circles are a big deal in Google+. They form the basis of your relationships with the people you interact with, and Google+ becomes a heck of a lot more fun when you use them well.

Once you have your Circles set up in a way that's good for you (Chapter 5 has more information on setting up Circles), it's time to put them to use. Here's how you share a post with a specific Circle:

1. **Click the Share what's new text box in the Stream.**

2. **By default the last Circles you used are active (the Public Circle to start with).** You can click the X icon next to a Circle name to remove it.

3. **Click Add more people and choose a Circle from the drop-down list that appears (as shown in Figure 6-13).** You can choose more than one Circle.

4. **If people in your Circles are not yet using Google+, an Also email X people not yet using Google+ check box appears (where X is the number of people).** Select it and Google+ sends an email to that person or people with your post.

5. **Click Share.**

FIGURE 6-13 Choosing Circles to share a post with.

The post is shared with people in your Circles (unless they have blocked you). Your post appears in their Stream as long as they have you in a Circle too. If they do not have you in a Circle, the post only appears if they click the Incoming link on the left-hand column. Unfortunately, you don't know if people have removed you from their Circles, so if you want to send an important message to a person, or people, then I suggest you do just that: send a message instead.

Although you can edit the content of the post afterward, you cannot change the Circle (or add new Circles) to a post once you have clicked Share. If you want to post the same post to a new Circle, you have to create a new post.

It is possible to view the people a post was shared with (in both your own posts and those by other people). If a post has been shared with a limited Circle or collection of Circles (that is, not the Public one) a small gray Limited link appears next to the post. Click Limited and a pop-up window appears displaying the people that the post was shared with (see Figure 6-14).

FIGURE 6-14 Discover who a post was shared with.

DO PEOPLE KNOW WHICH CIRCLE THEY'RE IN? Your Circles are private at all times. Nobody knows who else is in a Circle or what your Circles are called.

Managing Posts

Once you start to create multiple posts and add them to Google+, you may want to start managing your posts to some level.

Google+ offers a lot of options when it comes to managing posts. You can edit certain aspects of a post (although some aspects are permanent), delete posts, and manage or disable comments. It's also possible to prevent other people from resharing your posts.

CHANGING THE CONTENT OF A POST

You can change the content of a post and add new images, videos, and links (but not location information). Do the following to change a post:

1. **Click the small gray arrow to the right of a post and choose Edit this post (as shown in Figure 6-15).**

2. **You can change the content of the text in the text box and add images, video, and links.**

3. **Click Save.**

The post appears in the Stream with the updated text.

- -

DO PEOPLE KNOW IF I'VE EDITED A POST? Although there is no indication in your Stream that the post has been edited, other people see (Edited) next to the post along with the time that the post was edited. They cannot, however, see the contents of the original version.

- -

FIGURE 6-15 Editing a post.

Some people prefer to update their posts using the Comment text box below the original, rather than changing the post itself after it has been shared. On one level, this is a more honest edit; however, I think it's fine to edit a post up to a point. Once people have started to comment on your post, you might not want to edit it (or if you do, you should leave a comment stating that you have updated the post).

It is also possible to join in on the comments that other people make on your posts, in effect posting on your own post, rather than using the Edit this post function.

To comment on a post, do the following:

1. **Click Comment.**

2. **Type your update or thoughts.**

3. **Click Post comment.**

You can also +1 your own posts (which I think is somewhat egotistical, but if you really like what you said, it might be worth doing).

DELETING A POST

There may come a time (typically after a late night out or during a heated exchange) that you decide it's best to remove a post from Google+.

Fortunately, Google+ makes it easy to remove posts:

1. **Click the small gray arrow next to a post and choose Delete this post (as shown in Figure 6-16).**

2. **Click Delete.**

FIGURE 6-16 Deleting a post.

A message stating that your post has been deleted appears in your Stream, and the post vanishes from the Streams of the people you shared it with. A message appears in your Stream stating that your post has been deleted, but this does not appear in other people's Streams. If they've not read it, they'll never know it was there.

CAN I SEE MY DELETED POSTS? There is no way to view your posts once they have been deleted, and you cannot recover deleted posts, so be careful before clicking Delete.

DISABLING COMMENTS

One of the real joys of social networking is creating a really great, popular post and watching other people join the discussion.

Then there are the times when you don't want people to comment on your post, either because the post is by its nature inflammatory or because you don't feel that other people's comments are appropriate.

Google+ offers you a fair amount of tools for managing other people's comments (within reason — you can't change what other people think). But if you think people shouldn't be commenting at all on your post, you can disable comments completely:

1. **Write a post and choose which Circles to share it with.**

2. **Click Share.**

3. **Click the small gray icon to the right of the post and choose Disable comments (as shown in Figure 6-17).**

FIGURE 6-17 Disabling comments.

The post appears in other people's Streams as normal, but the Comment link is not present. You have to share a post first before disabling comments, so if you want to prevent comments at all, you should click it as soon as you've posted.

Sometimes you will create a post and not appreciate the comments that other people make on it. In this case you can remove or flag a comment. To manage comments like this, do the following.

1. **Move the mouse over the comment.** This brings up comment options, as shown in Figure 6-18.

2. **If you feel the comment is particularly offensive, you can report it to Google first by clicking the flag icon.** If you do this by accident, you can unflag the comment.

3. **Click the X icon to remove the comment from the post.**

4. **Click Delete.**

You can disable comments at any point, so if you don't want to keep deleting unwanted comments, you should use the Disable comments option. It is also possible to reenable comments by repeating the procedure and choosing Enable comments from the list.

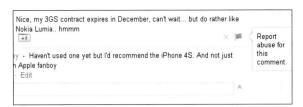

FIGURE 6-18 Removing comments from a post.

DISABLING RESHARE

Another thing you might want to consider is preventing people from resharing a post. By default, another person can share any post you write with people beyond your original Circle. Disabling resharing is great if you want to ensure that your post doesn't wander off into the ether. Do the following to disable resharing:

1. **Type your post and click Share.**

2. **Click the small gray arrow and choose Lock this post.** The first time you do this, you get the message shown in Figure 6-19.

3. **If you decide to allow sharing later, click the arrow again and choose Unlock this post.**

FIGURE 6-19 You get this message before locking a post so that it cannot be reshared.

The only indication a person gets that a post cannot be shared is the absence of the Share link underneath the post.

WHAT ABOUT CUT AND PASTE? There's nothing to stop people cutting the text from your post and sharing it themselves, although it comes from them and is not linked back to you. And hopefully, the lack of a reshare option encourages them not to do so. But if it really is that big a secret, then perhaps a social networking site is not the place to be writing it in the first place.

Managing Other People's Posts

It is also possible in Google+ to manage (albeit in a limited way) other people's posts. Click on the small gray arrow to the right of any post in your Stream to view the following options (as shown in Figure 6-20):

FIGURE 6-20 Managing other people's posts in your Stream.

+ **Link to this post.** Click this option to reveal a pop-up box with a URL linking directly to the post. This can be shared via email or on other social networking sites. If you want to share the post in Google+, it's easier to click Share below the post.

+ **Report abuse.** Click this option to report a post to Google. Four options are available: Spam, Nudity, Hate speech or violence, and Copyright. Choose the appropriate option and click Submit.

+ **Mute this post.** Click this option to remove the post from your Stream. This doesn't delete the post or remove it from other people's Streams. But it does ensure you can no longer see it.

+ **Block this person.** Click this option to block the person from your Google+ account.

While these options are more limited than for your own posts, they ensure you have some control over the content appearing in your Stream.

Related Questions

+ How do I manage my Circles? **CHAPTER 5, Adding People to Circles, Removing People from Circles**

+ What can I do if I no longer want to interact with people? **CHAPTER 5, Blocking People**

+ How can I manage my images in Google+? **CHAPTER 8, Uploading Photos and Creating Albums**

+ What does clicking +1 on a post do? **CHAPTER 10, Discovering What +1 Is All About**

CHAPTER SEVEN

HOW CAN I HANG OUT WITH MY FRIENDS USING GOOGLE+?

In this chapter:

+ Having a Live Text Chat in Google+
+ Setting Up Google Voice and Video
+ Adjusting Chat Settings
+ Having a Live Video and Audio Chat
+ Discovering What Hangouts Are All About

S haring posts with your friends and commenting on their posts is all well and good, but sometimes you want to reach out and talk to people directly.

Google+ is incredible for communication, going way beyond the messages and posts that you leave for friends on most social networks. Google has integrated its powerful communication tools, enabling you to have live chats (including text, audio, and video) with other people using Google+.

You can have live conversations in Google+ two distinct ways: Chat and Hangouts. Chat is a one-to-one communication tool, whereas Hangouts, Google's new and highly interactive group messaging service, enables you to talk to multiple people at once.

In this chapter, I show you how to use Google+ to communicate with friends.

Having a Live Text Chat in Google+

The quickest and easiest way to get in touch with a single person in Google+ is to use the built-in Chat functionality. Chat enables you to send text messages to someone and (as long as that person replies) get instant responses directly in the Google+ browser. In many respects, it's pretty similar to using an instant messaging service such as Windows Live Messenger or iChat. Once you've set up Google Voice and Video, you can also use it for live one-to-one video and audio conversations.

In the bottom of the left-hand column in the Home section of Google+, you can see the people with whom you can initiate chats. Unlike messages you post to people using Circles, Chat messages can only be initiated with people who have already approved you in Chat (which is separate from adding you to a Circle); and unless you already use it in one of Google's other services, such as Gmail, it's likely that nobody is listed here to begin with.

- -

SHOULD I USE CHAT OVER WINDOWS LIVE MESSENGER? I'd say yes. One of the upsides of using Google Chat over programs like iChat or Windows Messenger is that you don't need to install special client software to use it and can log in from any computer.

- -

The very first time you use Chat, you see a Send a message to text box and a list of available people (which may be currently empty), as shown in Figure 7-1.

Adding people to the Chat list requires you to enter their email addresses. Follow these steps:

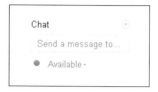

FIGURE 7-1 The Chat interface with an empty list.

1. **Click Send a message to and type the name of a person in your Google Contacts list.**

2. **Choose the correct email from the list of results.** If you do not have an email address in your Google Contacts, you need to type in the email address.

3. **Click Invite to chat.** A message appears saying the person will need to accept your invitation to chat and will have access to your email address (as shown in Figure 7-2).

4. **Click Send invite.** A yellow note appears saying your invitation has been sent successfully to the specific email address.

5. **Click the X button to remove the note, or wait a few seconds for it to disappear.**

FIGURE 7-2 You have to send an invitation to a person before you can use Chat.

The person who receives the invitation request sees a yellow note in Chat (as shown in Figure 7-3) saying you want to chat. The note also asks your friend if it is okay that his or her email address will be visible. If your friend clicks Yes, both of you will be able to initiate chats with each other.

When the person has accepted the invitation, that name appears in the Chat list. To the left of the name is an icon indicating a status. The following statuses can be displayed:

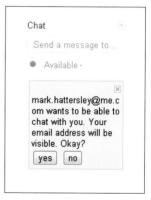

FIGURE 7-3 A Chat invitation being received.

🔘 Available for text chat

📹 Available for text and/or video chat

⬤ Busy

⊗ Offline or invisible

💬 In a conversation

🕐 Idle

📹 Idle (video enabled)

Click the name of a person to initiate a chat. A Chat window appears in the bottom-right of the Google+ interface (as shown in Figure 7-4). Type a text message in the box and press Enter or Return to send it to the other person.

If you find the Chat conversation window a little cramped, you can turn it into a larger window by clicking the pop-out icon at the top of the Chat window. Click Pop-in to return to a small window inside the web browser.

The person who receives your message hears a ping noise, and the text message

Pop-out icon

FIGURE 7-4 A Chat conversation.

appears in the same-style text box. From here, you can just keep typing messages and sending them back and forth. You don't need to wait for the other person to send a reply before sending another message.

- -

WHAT IF I WANT TO CHAT WITH A PERSON OFFLINE? If people are offline or idle, you can still send them a message. They will receive the message when they next log in to Google+.

- -

CHANGING YOUR CHAT STATUS

If you step away from your computer or log out of Google+, your Chat status changes first to idle, then to offline. However, it is possible to change your

Chat status in Google+ to indicate different states (as shown in Figure 7-5). Click Available (or whatever your current status is) and choose from the following list:

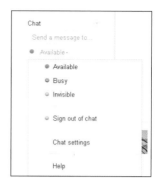

+ **Available.** The default status indicates that you are free to talk.

+ **Busy.** This status indicates that you aren't free to talk at the moment, but people can still send you messages.

+ **Invisible.** This status indicates to other people that you are offline. However, if they send you a message, you still receive it.

FIGURE 7-5 Changing your status in Chat.

+ **Sign out of chat.** This removes you from Chat completely (although you stay signed in to Google+). You do not receive any messages until you click Sign into chat.

It's fairly important to remember that indicating you are busy or invisible doesn't actually block incoming messages.

VIEWING CHAT HISTORY AND GOING OFF THE RECORD

One of the great things about Google Chat is that all your conversations are recorded so you can view them at a later date. All your chats in Google+ are saved in Gmail, which enables you to read through them as if they were an email conversation (as shown in Figure 7-6).

Do the following to take a look at your previous conversations:

1. **Click Gmail in the Google+ bar or go to http://mail.google.com.**

2. **Click Chat in the left-hand column (if it is not visible, click the More option at the bottom of the list, and it will be in the drop-down list).** The conversations you've had appear like Gmail messages in the main window.

3. **Click a message to opens its contents.**

You can even reply to previous chats as mail messages with the person. It's a great way to go over a previous conversation and pick up on an earlier thread.

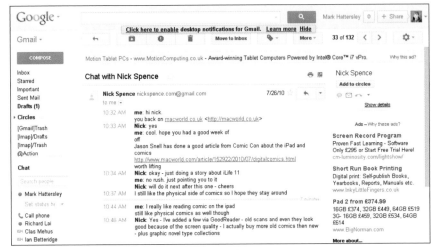

FIGURE 7-6 Viewing your Chat history in Gmail.

The conversation is recorded in your Gmail account and the account of the person you're talking to. Of course, you might not always want the other person to have a record of your conversation. In that case, you want to investigate Google Chat's off the record feature. This stops the things you say from being saved in Gmail.

To go off the record, in a Chat window click Actions and then click Go off the record. That part of the conversation does not appear inside the Chats section of Gmail. Both users see the message "You are now off the record" in their Chat boxes (as shown in Figure 7-7).

When you are finished with the private conversation, click Actions and click Go on the record to start recording the conversation again.

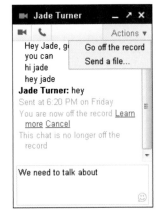

FIGURE 7-7 A conversation that is off the record.

HOW SECURE IS OFF THE RECORD? Although an off-the-record conversation does not appear in Gmail, that doesn't prevent the other person from using software to record the conversation. And the other person can still cut and paste the text.

Setting Up Google Voice and Video

It is also possible to have a live video (or just audio) conversation using Google+. This is a great way to keep in touch with people that's more personal than sending text messages.

There are two ways to have a video chat in Google+. The first is via the same one-to-one text message service that you looked at earlier in the chapter, and the second is via Hangouts (which you look at next). But before you can do either, you need to set up Google's Voice and Video plug-in on your computer (as shown in Figure 7-8). Do the following:

1. **Click the name of a person in the Chat section of the left-hand column.**
2. **Click the blue video icon in the top-left of the Chat window.**
3. **Click the Click here to add voice/video chat link.**
4. **Click Install voice and video chat.**
5. **Click Close.**

You can also install Voice and Video via Hangouts. Google+ prompts you to install the Google Voice and Video plug-in the first time you click Start a Hangout.

Google Voice and Video works with Google's Gmail, iGoogle (your personalized search page), and Orkut (an online networking site), so if you use other Google services, you may already have it installed on your system. You can also install the Google Voice and Video plug-in separately via the Voice and Video website (www.google.com/chat/video).

FIGURE 7-8 Installing the Google Voice and Video plug-in.

DO I NEED TO INSTALL GOOGLE VOICE AND VIDEO FOR EACH WEB BROWSER? No. You should only need to install Google Voice and Video once. Once the plug-in is installed on your system, it should work in all your different web browsers.

Adjusting Chat Settings

Once you have the Google Voice and Video plug-in installed, a set of options appear that enable you to adjust the settings (as shown in Figure 7-9). Access these by clicking the down-facing arrow next to Chat and choosing Settings. The following options are available:

+   **Verify your settings.** Click the + icon to reveal a video preview window and microphone and audio volume meters. Use these to check that your settings are working. If there's a problem, click Troubleshoot your settings.

+   **Camera.** If you have multiple cameras attached to your computer, you can choose which one to use here.

+ **Microphone.** You can select different audio input sources.

+ **Speakers.** Choose which speakers you wish to output audio to.

+ **Enable echo cancellation.** This check box (selected by default) prevents echo feedback caused by audio bouncing out of the speaker at one side and into the microphone.

+ **Enable high-resolution video.** This check box (unselected by default) enables higher-quality video but requires more bandwidth and can lead to performance issues.

+ **Report quality statistics to help improve voice and video chat.** This check box (selected by default) sends information to Google to help improve the video service.

+ **Play a sound notification when new chat messages arrive.** This check box (selected by default) plays a sound when you get a new message. This requires Flash to be installed in your web browser.

Click Save Changes or Cancel to return to Google+.

FIGURE 7-9 Google Voice and Video settings.

Having a Live Video and Audio Chat

It is possible to have video and audio chats in Google+ provided that your computer has a webcam attached to it, and most modern laptops and many desktops come with built-in webcams.

After you have the Voice and Video plug-in installed, initiating a video chat is similar to starting a text chat:

1. **Click the name of a person in the Chat list.**
2. **Click the blue video icon in the top-left of the Chat window.**
3. **The person has to click Answer.**

When you are connected, you see two video screens (as shown in Figure 7-10). The larger image is the person you are talking to, and the smaller one is how you look to the other person.

As with regular text chats, it is possible to get a larger video window by clicking the pop-out icon in the Chat window. This opens the text chat and a larger video window in a new screen.

You can also get a full-screen view (as shown in Figure 7-11) by hovering the mouse over the video window and clicking the full screen icon that appears in the top-right of the screen. Click the icon again in the top-right of the screen to return to windowed view.

It is also possible to mute the audio from the chat by clicking the microphone icon just below the video window.

Also note that you can continue to send text messages while having a video chat. This func-

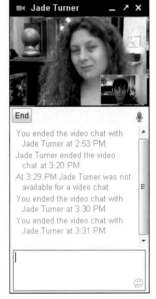

FIGURE 7-10 A video conversation in Google+.

tionality works as before. So it's possible to video chat while sending text and links to web pages in the regular text interface. Click End to finish the video chat when you're done.

- -

WHAT IF MY PORTRAIT WINDOW IS IN THE WAY? You can click and drag the smaller window and position it in any of the four corners. Hovering the mouse over the small video window also reveals a minimize icon that you can use to remove the smaller window from your window.

- -

FIGURE 7-11 Full-screen mode.

When a person attempts to initiate a video chat with you, Google+ makes a ringing noise and a text chat box (with a video screen) appears, as shown in Figure 7-12. Click Answer to initiate the call. Note that until you click Answer, you only see your own image in the video window, and the other person only sees hers.

FIGURE 7-12 Receiving a call.

- -

CAN I MAKE AN AUDIO CALL? Yes. Next to the video icon in the Chat window is a telephone icon. This initiates an audio call to the selected person. Audio calls work exactly the same way as video chats do but they are audio only.

- -

Discovering What Hangouts Are All About

With Google+'s video, audio, and text chat functionality, you might think you're all set for communication, but Google has an ace-in-the-hole feature called *Hangouts* that you really don't want to overlook.

Hangouts are like regular video chats, except they are group chats instead of one-to-one communications. You can invite multiple people to hang out, and they can come and go from the group as and when they like. As the name suggests, it's a great way for you and your friends to hang out while you are on your computers.

One of the great things about Hangouts is that there isn't the pressure of a direct video chat. You can just chill out with your friends while scrolling through the web or working on your computer.

You start a Hangout by doing the following:

1. **Click Start a hangout in the right-hand column.**

2. **By default Your circles is displayed in the Who do you want to hang out with? section (meaning that everybody will be invited).** You can remove Your circles and invite custom groups by clicking the X in Your circles.

3. **Click Add circles or people to share with.** Type the name of a Circle or person to include in the Hangout, as shown in Figure 7-13.

4. **Click Hang out.**

When you start the Hangout, you see a screen saying No one is here right now. This is because you need to wait for people to join the Hangout. As they join the Hangout, they appear in a row in the bottom of the screen, and you can take part in a group chat session.

When you are on the receiving end of an invitation to a Hangout, a link to join the group appears inside your Chat box (as shown in Figure 7-14). Click the link to open the Hangout window and click Hang out to join the group.

FIGURE 7-13 Starting a Hangout.

USING THE HANGOUT URL Hangouts open in separate web pages with individual URLs that are created for the Hangout and recycled into Google when you're done. You can share the URL outside of Google+, but only people logged in to Google+ and invited to the Hangout can join in.

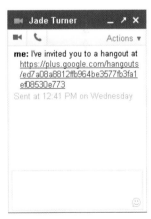

FIGURE 7-14 Joining a Hangout.

USING CONTROLS INSIDE HANGOUTS

Everybody inside the Hangout has access to the controls (as shown in Figure 7-15). They are as follows:

+ **Invite.** Use this button to invite extra people to the Hangout. Click Add circles or people to share with, and then add the name of a person or group in the sidebar that appears. Click Invite.

+ **Chat.** Click this button to bring up a text chat sidebar. Other users can see the text chat alongside the video chat. Note that they do not get any notification that you are sending text messages unless they click Chat.

+ **YouTube.** Click this button and the main window turns into a YouTube display. You can search for videos and play them in the main window. Other users can see these by clicking the YouTube icon. Any person in the Hangout can play or pause the YouTube video.

FIGURE 7-15 Controls inside a Hangout.

+ **Mute Video.** Click this button to remove your own video feed. You are still able to see other people in the Hangout.

+ **Mute Mic.** Click this button to turn off your mic. You are still able to hear other people in the Hangout.

+ **Settings.** Click this button to adjust the camera, microphone, and speaker settings while in a Hangout. The options are the same as outlined earlier in the chapter.

+ **Exit.** Click this button to leave a Hangout.

All people in the Hangout have equal access to the same controls; there's no leader or moderator of the group. Even if you originally set up the Hangout, you can't remove people, although you can leave at any time.

MUTING OTHER PEOPLE IN HANGOUTS

If you are unhappy with what a person is saying (or just want to keep someone quiet for a while) you can mute him:

1. **Hover your mouse over the person in the Hangout.**
2. **Click the Remote mute participant icon that appears.**
3. **Click Mute now in the menu bar that appears in the top of the screen.**
4. **Click Close (or wait for the menu bar to disappear).**

You are no longer able to hear the person you mute (although other people in the Hangout can still listen to him). To unmute a person, you follow the same action but click Cancel instead of Mute now.

BLOCKING SOMEONE IN HANGOUTS

If you don't like hanging out with someone, you can block her. Do this by performing the following:

1. **Hover your mouse over the person in the Hangout.**
2. **Click the red block person icon that appears.**
3. **Click Block.**

The person's video feed is replaced with a blank red screen and a no entry symbol (as shown in Figure 7-16). The blocked person sees you disappear from the Hangout (as if you'd exited it).

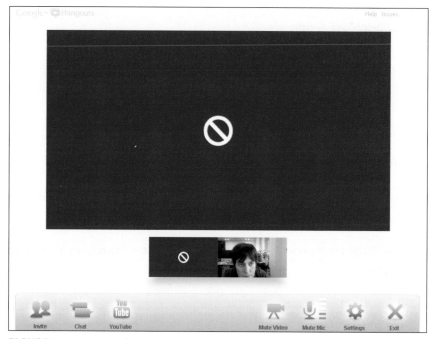

FIGURE 7-16 A person blocked in Hangouts.

The user that you've blocked is not rejected from the current Hangout (after all, that person may also be chatting to people who don't want to block him or her), but you and the other person are no longer able to see or talk to each other.

It's important to note that people you have blocked are not able to join a Hangout with you in future; they will get a message that a person in the Hangout has blocked them. And you won't be able to join a Hangout that already has a blocked person inside it.

A person you have blocked from Hangouts is removed from your Circles, and you are no longer able to chat with him, comment on his posts, or see each other's public posts. If you block people, they will find it difficult to communicate with you via Google+, which may be a good thing, but you should use it wisely and not on a whim.

If you change your mind and decide that you want to be able to talk to that person after all, you can unblock her. You cannot unblock a person in the Hangouts; instead, you do it through the Circles interface:

1. **Click the Circles icon.**

2. **Click More actions and choose View blocked.**

3. **Find the person in the list of blocked people and click Unblock.**

4. **Click Add to circles and choose a Circle to add the person to.**

5. **Click Done.**

You are now able to join Hangouts with that person again, as well as chat and comment on his posts (and that person is able to do the same with you). Chapter 5 has more information on Circles.

Related Questions

+ How do I find people on Google+? **CHAPTER 4, Searching for People You Know**

+ How do I create Circles of people to hang out with? **CHAPTER 5, Adding People to Circles**

+ How do I block and unblock people in Google+? **CHAPTER 5, Blocking People**

CHAPTER EIGHT

HOW DO I MANAGE AND UPLOAD PHOTOS IN GOOGLE+?

In this chapter:

+ Looking at Photos in Google+
+ Uploading Photos and Creating Albums
+ Uploading Photos on a Computer from an Android Phone
+ Editing and Sharing Photos in Lightbox
+ Editing Photos with the Creative Kit

One of the best aspects of social networking is being able to share all the great photos you've taken with friends. Google+ has fantastic photo-sharing features that enable you to upload, edit, organize, and share all your images with people in your Circles. Once you discover how comprehensive these features are, you'll wonder how you managed without them.

Google+ has a superb built-in display and exceptional photo-editing functionality. The website acts much more like a desktop photo-editing package than you'd expect.

Google+ also closely integrates with Google Android smartphones and tablets. Once Instant Upload is set up, any pictures you take on an Android mobile phone or tablet are instantly sent to your Google+ account, after which you can decide when and who to share them with.

Instant Upload is one killer feature of Google+ that enables you treat the service more like online storage (with no limit) for all the images you snap on your smartphone. But there's far more to Google+ photo editing than Instant Upload. In this chapter you learn how to upload, edit, and share your images using Google+.

Looking at Photos in Google+

To look at photos in Google+, click the photos icon in the menu bar. In the Stream you see a selection of images that have recently been uploaded from people in your Circles (as shown in Figure 8-1).

In the left-hand column you see the following options:

+ **Photos from your circles.** This option (the default) displays a montage of recently uploaded images in the Stream.

+ **Photos from your phone.** If you have a compatible phone set up to work with Google+ (I outline this later in the chapter), the images you have snapped on your phone appear here.

+ **Photos of you.** This option displays images that you (and other people) have indicated contain you.

+ **Photos from your posts.** This option displays the images that you have included in posts in your Stream.

+ **Your albums.** This option displays photos that you've organized into albums using Google+ and Google Picasa.

Hover your mouse over an image in a Google+ album and it expands slightly, and the album fans out to display the images contained within. Clicking an album opens all the images inside (click the Your albums link in the left-hand column again to return to the Your albums window).

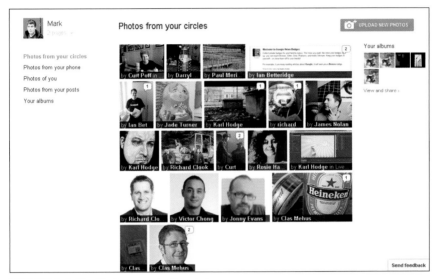

FIGURE 8-1 The Photos page in Google+.

HOW LONG DO MY IMAGES STAY ON GOOGLE? Google has set no limit to the number of images you can store on Google+, and the images remain as long as Google's photo service exists. As long as you're happy with Google+ storing all your images, you can use it as a free online cloud photo service from now on.

Uploading Photos and Creating Albums

Before you start using Google+ for sharing images, you need to get images on Google+. You can store as many images as you want on the service.

Follow these steps to add a photo to Google+ from your desktop:

1. **On the Photos page, click Upload New Photos.**

2. **If you're using Google Chrome, Safari, or Firefox, you can drag the desired image from your desktop to the Drag photos here part of the main window.** Alternatively, click Select photos from your computer, locate the image, and click Open.

3. **Wait for the photo to upload to Google+ (a load bar graphic runs under the image).** The image loads in an album named after today's date (as shown in Figure 8-2).

4. **Give the album a new title using the Album name box.** To send the images to a preexisting album, click add to an existing album and choose one from the drop-down list.

5. **If you hover your mouse over an image that has been uploaded, four icons appear.** These are Rotate left, Rotate right, Edit, and Delete. You learn about editing images later in the chapter.

6. **Click Create album (or Add photos if you're adding to an existing album).**

FIGURE 8-2 Uploading images to Google+.

TAGGING PHOTOS

Google+ has pretty impressive face-recognition technology built in. If Google+ spots a face in the image you upload, a window appears, enabling you to tag the people in the photograph (as shown in Figure 8-3). *Tagging* is connecting a person's name to a face in a photograph.

To tag a person, do the following:

1. **Click a person (or multiple images of the same person) in the left side of the tagging window.**

2. **Type the name of the person in the text box in the right.** As you type a person's name, a list of people appears. Select the right person and click Tag.

3. **You can tag multiple people in this window by repeating Steps 1 and 2.**

4. **Click Done tagging when you're finished.**

You can skip the tagging process by clicking Skip tagging at any point.

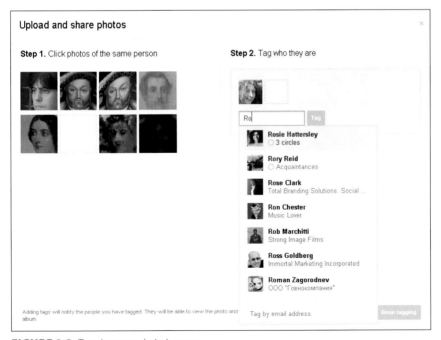

FIGURE 8-3 Tagging people in images.

SHARING ALBUMS WITH CIRCLES

After you upload photos, Google+ prompts you to share the new album with your Circles. Type a comment and then click Add circles or people to share with and choose the desired people. Click Share to post the new album to your Stream. If you click Cancel, the album is still created, but the images are only available to you (a red icon appears underneath the album image in Your albums).

CAN I CHANGE THE NAME OF AN ALBUM? Yes. Click Photos and Your albums, and then click an album to display the photos. If you click the album title in this window, you can edit the text.

Once your images have been uploaded, you can look at them by clicking Your albums in the left-hand column and clicking the name of your album. The images appear as a montage with a selection of options (as shown in Figure 8-4).

Here are some options available on this screen:

+ **Share album.** It's possible to share an album by clicking Share album, typing the name of a person or Circle, and clicking Share.

+ **Options.** This drop-down list contains two options: Share album via link (which provides a URL link to share) and Delete album.

+ **Add More Photos.** You can add more images to an album by clicking this button.

+ **Visible to.** This displays the Circles and people that the album is shared with. To the right is the number of photos in the album and the date that it was uploaded.

You can slightly expand the size of the images in the window by hovering your mouse over them. Click on an image to view it alongside a selection of additional controls called *Editing* and *Sharing*. Click the X button to return to the Photos window.

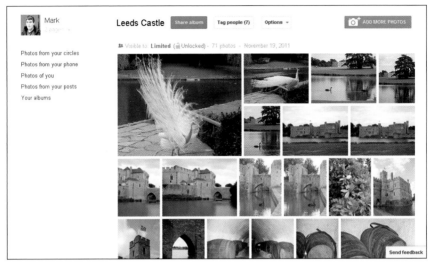

FIGURE 8-4 Viewing images in an album.

CHANGING SHARING OPTIONS AND LOCKING ALBUMS

It is possible to change the sharing options of an album and lock your photos to prevent them from being shared. Follow these steps:

1. **Click the Visible to: Limited link to display which Circles you currently share with.**

2. **Add and remove Circles and individuals by clicking Add more people.**

3. **To lock the album, select the Lock this album check box.**

4. **Click Save.**

A few things happen when you lock an album:

+ New name tags created by others become text tags (although, as the owner, you're still able to tag your photos).

+ No one is able to +1 the photos.

+ All posts about the album are also locked (including posts created before the album was locked).

You can unlock an album by repeating the preceding steps and deselecting the Locked album check box.

Uploading Photos on a Computer from an Android Phone

If you have a Google Android-based smartphone, you can upload images from it directly to Google+.

You can learn about the mobile versions of Google+ in Chapter 13, but if you own an Android-based phone and use it as a camera, you might want to investigate the Instant Upload feature. It sends any photographs you take on your mobile phone directly to Google+, where you can share them at your leisure.

First you need to download the Google+ app from Google Play, formerly called the Android Market. On your Android phone do the following:

1. **Tap the Market app (Google Play) icon on your phone.**

2. **Tap the search icon in the top-right and enter Google+ into the Search Google Play box.** Tap the search icon again.

3. **Tap the Google+ app (it should be at the top of the list).**

4. **Tap Install.** You may be asked to enter your password at this point.

5. **Tap Accept & download.**

Once you have the Google+ app installed, you need to enable Instant Upload:

1. **Tap Open from the Market app if you've just installed Google+; otherwise open the app from the Applications folder.**

2. **If this is the first time you've launched Google+, select an account from the list to sign in.** It has to be the same account that you use to sign in to Google+.

3. **The first time you launch Google+, you are presented with an Enable Instant Upload screen with three options (as shown in Figure 8-5):**

FIGURE 8-5 Enable Instant Upload in Google+.

+ Over Wi-Fi or mobile network

+ Over Wi-Fi only

+ Disable Instant Upload

4. **Choose the option you want (be careful with using the default Wi-Fi or mobile network option if you take a lot of photos, as the upload can eat up your data allowance).** Tap Continue.

If you are already using Google+, then you need to enable Instant Upload in the settings (there are some extra options here that are also worth investigating):

1. **Open the Google+ app.**

2. **Press the Menu button on the phone and click Settings.**

3. **Scroll down to Enable Instant Upload and select the check box.**

4. **Tap When to upload photos and choose Over Wi-Fi or mobile network or Over Wi-Fi only.**

5. **The Roaming uploads check box is unselected by default.** I recommend leaving it this way unless you want to incur significant data charges when using your mobile phone on a different network than usual (such as when you are traveling).

6. **The On battery check box is selected by default; this ensures that photos are uploaded when you are using the battery.** The Instant Upload feature is far less useful if this box isn't selected.

7. **If you want all the pictures currently on the device to upload to Google+, tap Upload all photos.**

8. **Press the Back button to return to the Google+ app.**

With the Instant Upload feature enabled, any photo you take on your Android phone (using the default camera app) instantly syncs with Google+. To see a picture taken on your Android phone in Google+, click the photos icon and choose Photos from your phone.

Google+ displays a slide show of photos taken from your camera (as shown in Figure 8-6).

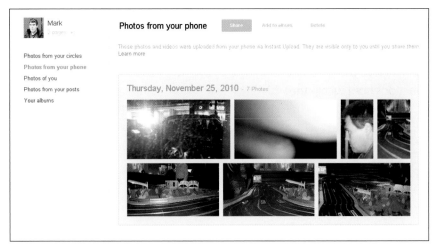

FIGURE 8-6 Photos from your phone.

All the images you have uploaded or taken from the phone appear in the Stream and are organized by date. By default they are not visible to anybody else on Google+; they are just stored online, ready for you to share. You can click and highlight images in the window, and three options are available:

+ **Share.** Click Share to share the images with your Circles. Add a comment, choose which Circles to share with, and click Share.

+ **Add to album.** Click this to add the photos to your photo albums. You can type the name of a new album or click Add to an existing album and choose one from the drop-down list. When you create an album, a Share window appears (you can click Cancel just to add the images to an album).

+ **Delete.** Click Delete and Okay to remove the selected images from Google+. The images are not deleted from your mobile phone.

Normally, clicking an image in Photos takes you to a Lightbox view of that image, meaning the screen turns dark so you can better view the photo, and photo editing, comments, and sharing controls appear. Because clicking on an image in Photos from your phone selects the image, you need to double-click on the image (or click the small + icon in the bottom-right of the window) to enter Lightbox mode.

Editing and Sharing Photos in Lightbox

Google+ has a surprisingly competent image-editing mode called *Lightbox* that enables you take a closer look at pictures and perform a wide range of functions from within the web browser (as shown in Figure 8-7).

FIGURE 8-7 Looking at a photo in Lightbox.

Lightbox enables you to tag people, share images, add comments, perform edits, add captions, view photo details, download photos, and more. Click on any photo to view it in Lightbox.

The image you click on appears in the main window against a black background that makes it easier to view. On the left and right of the screen are navigation arrows that enable you to move between different images in an album (clicking on the image also moves to the next photo in the album). Click View All at the bottom of Lightbox to reveal a slide show of all the preview images, enabling you to skip to any photo in an album.

- -

CAN I EDIT OTHER PEOPLE'S PHOTOS? No. Lightbox only enables you to edit your own images. You can, however, download photos from other people, upload them to your own photo library, and then edit them.

- -

ADDING COMMENTS TO PHOTOS

You can add comments to a photo in Lightbox mode by using the Comments sidebar on the right (as shown in Figure 8-8). Type a comment and click Post comment, and it'll be visible to anybody looking at the image. Also, anybody else looking at the image can use the Comments bar to add comments.

The comments appear next to that particular photo, not the entire album. In the Photos window, a small speech bubble with a number inside indicates how many comments each photo has received.

Google+ enables you to manage and delete comments in the Photos window:

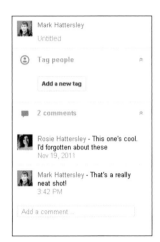

FIGURE 8-8 Lightbox comments.

1. **Click Options (to the right of View All) and choose Manage comments.** Delete and report icons appear next to each comment.

2. **Click the delete icon (the X) next to a comment you wish to remove.** If you click the report icon (the flag), you delete the comment and alert Google to investigate the contents.

You can delete your own comments from a photo at any time by clicking the Delete button that appears below the comments.

- -

CAN I HIDE COMMENTS? It's possible to hide the Comments sidebar by clicking the gray vertical bar that divides the main photo from the comments. This only hides it for you, though; other people can still add comments on the photo.

- -

ADDING DESCRIPTIONS TO PHOTOS

You can give your photos descriptions in Lightbox mode by clicking Edit next to Untitled at the top of the captions column and typing some text into

the box that appears (as shown in Figure 8-9).
Click Add description to add the text to the
photograph.

You can delete a caption by selecting the text
again and deleting it.

EDITING PHOTOS IN LIGHTBOX

It is also possible to perform basic edits in
Lightbox mode using the buttons at the top of
the screen (as shown in Figure 8-10). Click Edit
and the following options are available:

+ **Rotating images.** Use the left and
  right icons to quickly rotate an image 90
  degrees in either direction.

+ **Auto-fix.** Click the auto-fix icon (magic
  wand) to enable Google+ to adjust parts
  of the image, such as contrast, saturation,
  and so on. I find auto-fix does a pretty
  good job of improving a picture. The
  changes aren't permanent, and you can
  undo them at any time by selecting the
  same menu option.

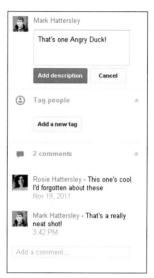

FIGURE 8-9 Adding a caption to a photo in Lightbox.

FIGURE 8-10 The Edit
options in Lightbox mode.

+ **Creative Kit.** Click this option to open a more detailed editing mode.

Editing Photos with the Creative Kit

The Google+ Creative Kit enables you to customize your images, adding a
wide range of visual effects that can improve and transform pictures, as well
as some playful effects that can be fun to use.

To edit an image with the Creative Kit, open the image in Lightbox mode,
and then click Creative Kit. This opens the image in a new window offering a
wide range of controls (as shown in Figure 8-11).

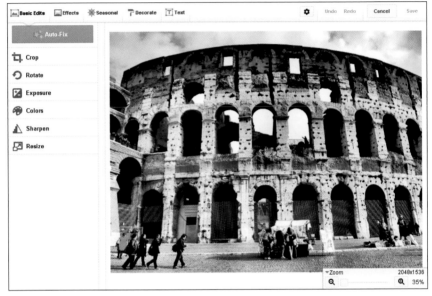

FIGURE 8-11 The Creative Kit.

At the top of the screen sits a selection of options:

+ **Basic Edits.** These enable you to crop, rotate, and adjust the image.

+ **Effects.** A wide range of effects can be added to an image, as well as some more specialized functions such as Blemish Fix.

+ **Seasonal.** Fireworks, Santa beards, Christmas hats, snowflakes, and other holiday-related items can all be added from here.

+ **Decorate.** Stickers, speech bubbles, fake beards, masks, and hats can all be found here.

+ **Text.** Add text to an image.

Some other functions are worth looking at here too. Click the settings icon (the small gear) and choose Fullscreen to edit in full screen mode. And you can zoom in on an image using the Zoom slider in the bottom-right of the photo (when zoomed in, you can click and drag an image using a Hand tool).

You can reverse any changes you make by clicking Undo. You can click Undo multiple times to remove any unwanted effects. Clicking Redo reapplies the effect.

BASIC EDITS

Under the Basic Edits menu are a number of commands worth looking at. At the top is a large red Auto-Fix button that performs the same function as auto-fix in Lightbox mode.

Below that are six interesting tools that perform more detailed edits: Crop, Rotate, Exposure, Colors, Sharpen, and Resize.

Crop

The Crop tool enables you to remove parts of the image and focus on just the part that you want.

1. **Click Crop to overlay a crop box on the image (as shown in Figure 8-12).**

2. **Resize the crop box by dragging the four drag handles at the corners of the box.** You can also move the box around by clicking and dragging inside the square.

3. **Click the Constraints drop-down list to choose a specific proportion for the image.** There are a wide range of options, including Square and Golden Ratio. Scroll down the list and you also see sizes for popular websites, including Twitter, Blogger, and YouTube, as well as the correct constraints for different desktops and even the iPhone.

4. **You can resize the image to precision by typing numbers into the Actual size boxes for width and height.**

5. **Select the Scale Photo check box and the image remains the same size in pixels, but it is zoomed in to the crop-area of the image in the box.** Note that you lose some image quality from scaling up the image.

6. **Click Apply when you're happy with the cropped image.**

FIGURE 8-12 The Crop tool.

Rotate

The Rotate tool enables you to turn an image on a circular axis. In Creative Kit you can also flip an image horizontally and vertically. Five options are available:

+ Rotate left 90 degrees
+ Rotate right 90 degrees
+ Flip horizontally
+ Flip vertically
+ Straighten

Dragging the Straighten slider overlays a square grid on the image. Moving the Straighten slider left rotates the image left up to 45 degrees, and moving the slider right rotates the image right up to 45 degrees (as shown in Figure 8-13).

FIGURE 8-13 Using the Straighten slider on a photo.

WHAT IF I WANT TO ROTATE AN IMAGE BY MORE THAN 45 DEGREES? You can use the rotate left or rotate right button to rotate the image 90 degrees; then you use the Straighten slider to move it back to a rotation between 45 and 90 degrees until you get the desired effect.

Exposure

This Exposure tool enables you to adjust elements of the exposure in an image. Click the Exposure button to reveal four sliders (as shown in Figure 8-14):

+ Exposure
+ Highlights
+ Shadows
+ Contrast

Move the sliders until you're happy with the look of your image and click Apply to place the changes.

Colors

You can adjust the color of an image (to a certain extent) using the Colors options (as shown in Figure 8-15). Four options are available:

+ **Auto-Colors.** Click this button for automatic color adjustments.

+ **Neutral Picker.** Click this button and an eyedropper tool appears. Use it to click on a neutral (usually gray) part of an image to help set the color balance. You can click multiple times until you get the effect you're after.

FIGURE 8-14 Adjusting the Exposure.

FIGURE 8-15 Using the Neutral Picker tool to adjust the color.

+ **Saturation.** Use this slider to increase the vibrancy of colors.

+ **Temperature.** Use this slider to increase or decrease the warmth of colors in an image.

Click Apply to apply the changes.

Sharpen

You can adjust the sharpness of an image (within reason, blurry pictures remain blurry) using the Sharpen tools. Three main tools are available:

+ Sharpness

+ Clarity

+ Unsharp Mask

Clicking Unsharp Mask brings up another set of controls (as shown in Figure 8-16) that enable you to adjust fine control within a set area:

+ **Radius.** Drag this slider to set how many pixels next to each other will be sharpened by the effect.

+ **Strength.** Drag this slider to set how pronounced the sharpness will be.

+ **Clarity.** Drag this slider to set how clear the image will be.

Click Apply when you're happy with the effect.

Resize

You can resize an image to make it larger or smaller using the New dimensions boxes (as shown in Figure 8-17). Type the required size (in pixels) using the width and height text boxes.

FIGURE 8-16 Using the Unsharp Mask.

You can select two check boxes:

+ **Use Percentages.** This changes the width
  and dimensions boxes to represent the
  percentage size difference (with 100 percent being the default). You can make an
  image larger by entering an amount such
  as 200 to make it twice the size.

+ **Keep Proportions.** This ensures that the
  image stays proportionally the same in
  width and height. As you enter new width
  or height numbers, the corresponding
  box will have the appropriate amount
  entered automatically.

Click Apply when you're happy with the
changes.

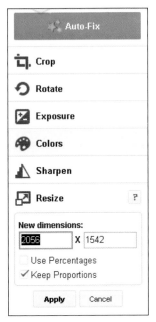

EFFECTS

FIGURE 8-17 Resizing
an image.

The Effects menu offers different visual tech-
niques that you can add to an image (as shown in Figure 8-18). The effects are
split into the following categories:

+ **Google+ Exclusives.** This category includes a wide range of effects
  such as Polaroid Plus and Reala 400 as well as color effects such as Sun
  Aged and Magenta Fade.

+ **Basics.** These are simple but often powerful effects such as Black and
  White, Boost, and Soften.

+ **Camera.** There are a range of camera effects here, including Lomo-ish,
  HDR-ish, CinemaScope, and 1960's.

+ **Color.** Here you find specific color effects such as Duo-Tone, Heat Map
  2.0, and Cross Process.

+ **TouchUp.** These tools are particularly good at fixing images. On most of them, you implement the effect by drawing on the image with a Brush tool. Effects include Blemish Fix, Airbrush, and Shine-Be-Gone.

Most of the effects are implemented using a range of sliders, drop-down lists, and the color picker to adjust the image.

FIGURE 8-18 Using the Effects window to add a black-and-white effect.

DECORATE

Some of the more wacky effects are in the Decorate menu. Here you can drag and drop effects onto the image to create something wacky (see Figure 8-19).

Google adds new effects to the Decorate menu all the time. When you drag and drop a sticker effect to an image (like my duck with a speech bubble), it appears with four drag handles, enabling you to adjust the size of the effect. A window appears with options for the sticker (as shown in Figure 8-20).

FIGURE 8-19 Livening up an image with the Decorate option.

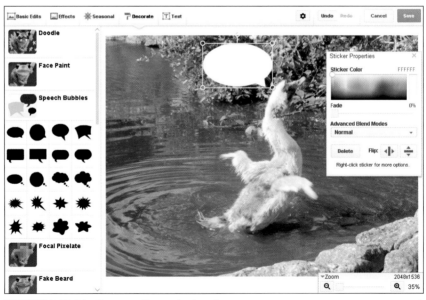

FIGURE 8-20 The Decorate Properties interface.

TEXT

It is also possible to overlay text on an image (as shown in Figure 8-21) by doing the following:

1. **Open an image in the Creative Kit and click Text.**

2. **Type the desired words into the text box in the top-left of the screen.**

3. **Choose a font from the list provided.**

4. **Click Add.** The text appears in the middle of the image. You can move it around and adjust the size using the four drag handles (as shown in Figure 8-22).

5. **Adjust the color of the text by clicking in the Font Color box in the Text Properties window.**

FIGURE 8-21 The options for adding text to an image.

FIGURE 8-22 Adding and repositioning text on the image.

6. **Drag the Fade slider to the right to blend the text into the image.** You can select a range of Blend modes from the Advanced Blend Modes drop-down list.

7. **Use the bold, italic, and justification icons to adjust text.**

8. **Adjust the size of the text using the Size slider.**

9. **Use the flip icons to flip the text.**

10. **Click anywhere on the image to remove the Text Properties box (you can reclick the text to bring it back up).** The text is already added to the image, so there is no Apply button.

You can also right-click the text to bring up further text options, including Straighten and Remove Distortion. You can remove text by right-clicking it and choosing Delete Type from the drop-down list.

USING PICASA WITH IMAGES

Google+ enables you to implement a wide range of visual effects to your photographs. But one of the really great things about using photos in Google+ is that the account is also automatically linked to Google's photo-management service called *Picasa*.

You can download the most current version of Picasa for Windows and Mac from http://picasa.google.com. This program syncs with Google+ and enables you to add even more effects to images and manage them with greater finesse.

You can also use a web-based version of Picasa at https://picasaweb. google.com/home. This service enables you to work with images to a greater depth online than Google+. And any changes you make in Picasa are automatically synced with your Google+ account.

Related Questions

+ How do I attach photos of me to my profile? **CHAPTER 2, Adding More Photographs of Yourself**

+ How do photos appear in my Stream? **CHAPTER 3, Viewing Photos**

CHAPTER NINE

HOW DO I DISCOVER INTERESTING NEWS SUBJECTS?

In this chapter:

+ Discovering "What's Hot" Information
+ Looking at Ripples
+ Searching for Information

On Google+, not only can you look at posts from people in your Circles but you can also browse posts from people you may never have met. This is all part of Google+'s open nature: you can share content publicly or privately using Circles.

Google's core strength is its powerful search technology, which is baked right into Google+. Google even integrates web articles that weren't originally posted on Google+ in the form of Sparks. You can view these news snippets (or sparks of information) on Google+. And you can use Google+ tools to narrow your searches and save these searches to the left-hand column for easy access. All this makes it much easier for you to move beyond your friends and follow people from around the world who have interesting stories to tell.

Discovering "What's Hot" Information

Probably the best way to get started looking at news on Google+ is to use the What's hot feature.

Click What's hot in the left-hand column of the home page. This automatically brings up a list of popular posts in the Stream that Google+ users are +1ing, sharing, and commenting on (as shown in Figure 9-1). It's a great way to quickly see what's going on in the world beyond your Circles.

FIGURE 9-1 Looking at What's hot on Google+.

You can comment on stories, share them on your own Stream, and +1 the ones you like.

CAN I CUSTOMIZE THE WHAT'S HOT NEWS? Not really. What's hot is designed to show what's popular on Google+ rather than reflect your own interests and tastes. You can use search tools (which I discuss later in the chapter) to find more personalized content.

Looking at Ripples

One incredibly cool feature of Google+ that often goes unnoticed is Ripples. This is a diagram that shows how a story has spread throughout Google+ over time.

It's particularly satisfying if something you post goes viral because you can visually witness how it spreads throughout the Google+ network.

To look at the Ripples, click the small arrow icon in the top-right corner of a news story and choose View Ripples. This opens a new window displaying a graphic of the story, as shown in Figure 9-2.

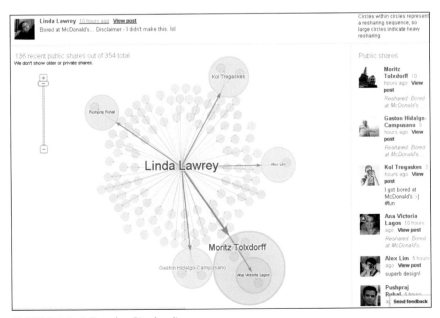

FIGURE 9-2 A Google+ Ripples diagram.

The Ripples diagram consists of a number of circles with arrows pointing between them. The name of the person who originally created the post is in the middle, and the circles surrounding it are other people who shared it. These circles vary in size and have circles within them that represent the number of times the post has been reshared; therefore, the larger circles represent people who have had a lot of reshares.

The graphic is interactive (it works similar to Google Maps). You can zoom in and out using the slider on the left side, and click on and drag the image around to view the different circles. If you hover your mouse over a person's name, you see his or her post sharing the Ripple, and if you click a circle, you see the comments made by people sharing that post in the right-hand column (as shown in Figure 9-3).

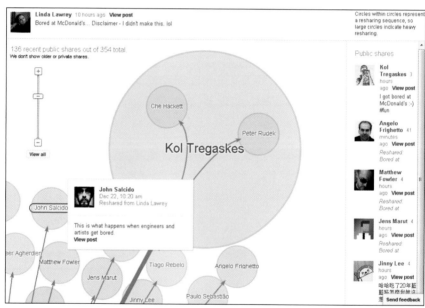

FIGURE 9-3 Checking out circles in a Ripple.

Below the circles graphic is a timeline where you can see how a post spreads over time (as shown in Figure 9-4). To the left of the graph is a number showing the maximum number of shares by a single person, and the names of some sharers appear throughout.

The graph below the Ripples diagram isn't interactive, but below the graph is a time slider you can use to view the circle as it progresses over time. A really neat trick is to drag the slider all the way to the left and click Play, and then watch the Ripples diagram grow as it develops over time.

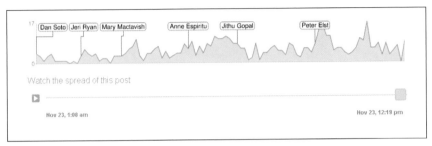

FIGURE 9-4 A timeline of how a post has spread.

Below the timeline are three sets of data about the post that you can use for further information:

+ **Influencers.** This is a list of the top five people who shared a post, and got the most public reshares. This is a useful way to find influential people.

+ **Statistics.** This list displays the following statistics on a publicly shared post:

　+ **Avg. chain length.** The average number of people who shared the link one after another.

　+ **Longest chain.** The highest number of people who shared the link one after another in a straight line.

　+ **Shares/Hour.** The average number of times the link was shared in an hour.

+ **Languages.** This pie chart shows the different languages used to share the post.

Above all, I find Ripples a great way to discover interesting and influential people. It's also gratifying to see how my posts have spread. Clicking View Ripples is particularly useful if you're running a Google+ Page for a business or brand and want metric information on how your posts are doing. (Chapter 16 has more information on using Google+ to promote a brand.)

CAN I VIEW RIPPLES ON MY OWN POSTS? Yes. You can view Ripples on any public post that has been reshared. Click the arrow in the top-right of the post and look for View Ripples.

Searching for Information

Another highly useful way to use Google+ as an information source is to use its built-in search functionality. You can use this search feature to create custom news feeds and save them to the left-hand column for easy access.

This great Google+ feature becomes almost like a personalized version of Google News (or perhaps similar in function, if you've used it, to Google Reader).

Start by typing a search term into the Search Google+ text box at the top of the screen. You can search for vague topics like **technology, fashion,** or **football,** or more specific subjects like **robotics** or **genetics.** You can search for specific stories that are happening in the news, such as **Egypt protests,** or new products you're interested in, like **iPhone 5.** In fact, you can search for just about anything you find interesting. Press Enter or Return to perform the Google+ search.

The results of your search appear in the Stream, as shown in Figure 9-5. As you look at the Stream, new stories appear at the top, which most of the time is fine, but if you're searching for a popular topic, it can get distracting. You can stop Google+ from adding new stories to the Stream by clicking the Pause icon in the Stream. Click Play if you want to resume live updating.

NARROWING YOUR SEARCH

By default, Google+ includes posts from all of Google+ and articles from the wider Internet (which Google+ refers to as Sparks). You can focus on different areas using the two drop-down lists below the search term. You can choose from the following:

+ **Everything**
+ **People and pages**
+ **Google+ posts**

+ **Sparks**

+ **Hangouts**

FIGURE 9-5 Searching for news.

If you're using Everything, Google+ posts, or Hangouts, a second drop-down list enables you to narrow the search:

+ **From everyone**

+ **From your circles**

+ **From you**

Underneath the Everything, From everyone, and From Everywhere narrowing functions are two further options (as shown in Figure 9-6):

+ **Most recent.** The most recent items matching the search term appear first.

+ **Best of.** The highest trending or most popular posts and Sparks top the list.

Use these options to get a variety of different search results in the Stream.

Google

Google+ posts ▼   From your circles ▼

Most recent   Best of

FIGURE 9-6 Narrowing your search.

SAVING SEARCHES

You can save a search term for quick access. Click Save this search and it appears under What's hot in the left-hand column (as shown Figure 9-7). Now when you want to search for posts on that search term, just click it in the left-hand column and it is entered automatically into the search text box.

To remove a search term from the left-hand column, hover your mouse over it and click the X icon that appears.

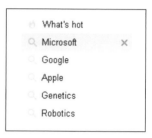

What's hot

Microsoft   ×

Google

Apple

Genetics

Robotics

FIGURE 9-7 Saved searches in the left-hand column.

- -

IF I SAVE A SEARCH, DOES IT SAVE THE OPTIONS? Going to a saved search always takes you back to the default Everything and From everyone options, even if you've saved the search term using different settings.

- -

Trends

Dancing with the Stars
Breaking Dawn
Groupon
Justin Bieber
Mitt Romney
Santa Claus
Martin Scorsese
Jason Segel
Egypt
Major League Baseball

FIGURE 9-8 Trending topics.

TRENDING INFORMATION

One thing that Google+ has integrated into Search is Trends. Whenever you search for a news story, you see Trends appear in the right-hand column, as shown in Figure 9-8. These Trends are topics that people are searching for in Google+ at that moment. Click a trending topic to automatically use that as a search term.

IS THIS THE SAME AS GOOGLE TRENDS? No. Google also has a product called *Google Trends* (www.google.com/trends) that shows trending topics from its search engine. Google Trends displays different results.

Related Questions

+ How do I search for people? **CHAPTER 4, Searching for People You Know**

+ How do I add people I've found to my Circles? **CHAPTER 5, Adding People to Circles**

+ How Do I Reshare Posts? **CHAPTER 6, Choosing Which Circles to Share Your Posts With** and **CHAPTER 10, Recommending Articles and Posts With +1**

CHAPTER TEN

WHAT IS +1 AND HOW DO I USE IT WITH GOOGLE+?

In this chapter:

+ Discovering What +1 Is All About
+ Recommending Articles and Posts with +1
+ Integrating +1 with Your Website
+ Managing Your +1 Web Content in Google+

I f you are familiar with Facebook, you are well aware of the concept of clicking a Like button. And you won't be surprised that Google+ has a similar function called +1.

Clicking Google's +1 button is a quick way for you to indicate approval of a post, image, article, or comment on Google+ (or the wider web) and to give it wider exposure. Clicking the +1 button is a great way to recommend items, give advice to your friends, and start conversations.

Furthermore, +1 also enables you to share items you find on the web inside your Stream in Google+. So you can quickly use +1 to populate your Stream with the interesting content you find during your web travels.

Discovering What +1 Is All About

The great thing about having a +1 button rather than a Like button is that it doesn't necessarily mean that you approve the post (although most of the time that's what it implies). I've seen people post the death of a loved one on Facebook, and other people click Like, which is a rather odd way of passing on condolences.

But +1 is more generic, and it adds your name to the group of people who want to associate themselves with a post or web page. It isn't, however, another form of the Share icon. You still need to share content for it to appear in your Stream.

Google has integrated +1 with many of its services, such as Google Search, YouTube, and Google Reader. And people can add the +1 icon to their websites, which enables users to like and share web pages with Google+ directly from a website (as shown in Figure 10-1).

Content that you have +1'd can appear on your profile, although it's not publicly available by default. Later in the chapter I show you how to increase the visibility of your +1 content so other people can easily see your interests. It's also a great way of keeping track of things you like, and you can always check up on them later (I use it as a form of long-term bookmarking for pages I've found interesting).

Finally, when you use +1, you're helping the websites you like get better results from Google Search. Every time you +1 a page, Google takes that into account in its search results, and when you use Google Search you'll find that people in your Circles who liked particular websites appear next to the search results.

FIGURE 10-1 The +1 button integrated with a website.

Recommending Articles and Posts with +1

Using +1 to recommend a post in Google+ is straightforward: Click the +1 button at the bottom of a post. The button turns blue to indicate that you have clicked it and a counter appears below, listing the number of people who have also +1'd that article (as shown in Figure 10-2).

If you are the only person to have +1'd an article, it says "You +1'd this." Click the counter and a box appears displaying the people who also +1'd the article (as shown in Figure 10-3).

It is possible to deselect the +1 button (if you've clicked it by accident) by clicking it a second time.

You can also use +1 to show you like comments on posts, as well as the posts themselves. Hover your mouse over a comment to reveal the +1 button. The first comment always appears on a post, but clicking Comments on a post reveals the comments people have made.

FIGURE 10-2 Google+ displays people that have +1'd a post.

FIGURE 10-3 Other people who have +1'd a post.

As you use Google+ (and other Google services) you'll discover the +1 button distributed liberally throughout various areas. For example, you can +1 a photo. Click the photos icon and click on an image to open it, and you'll see the +1 button on the bottom-right (as displayed in Figure 10-4). Chapter 8 has more information on adding and managing photos.

You'll also find Google +1 at the bottom of many web pages. This enables you to like and post on the page directly, without having to cut and paste the page into Google+ manually (you need to be signed in on Google during that web browsing session).

When you click the +1 button on an external web page, an extra option to share the page on your Google+ Stream appears.

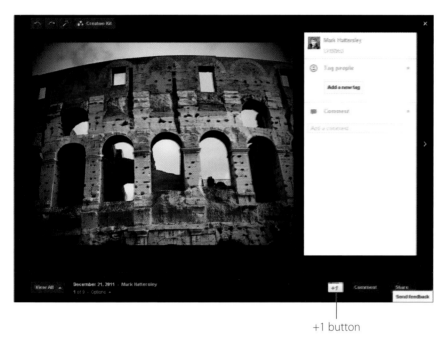

+1 button

FIGURE 10-4 Use +1 to like photos.

You can also share links from external websites using the +1 button. Click the +1 button first and then click the Share on Google+ text box to open a wider interface (as shown in Figure 10-5). Use the Circles options at the bottom to remove and add groups, and click Share.

You'll also find the +1 button integrated into Google News (http://news. google.com). If you are listed as the author of a news article, Google includes a link to your Google+ page with the story (as shown in Figure 10-6). You can add these people by hovering over the profile photo and selecting the appropriate Circle from the Add to circles menu.

And if people in your Circles have +1'd a news story, their photos appear beside the story.

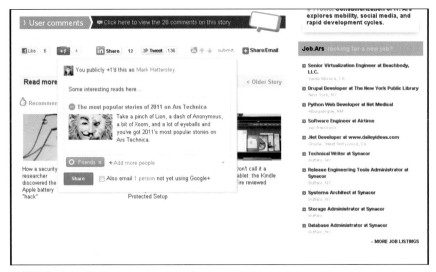

FIGURE 10-5 Sharing a page using +1.

FIGURE 10-6 Google+ profile photos appear next to articles people have written in services like Google News.

You can also find +1 integrated with Google Reader, although as far as I can see, it doesn't have the same profile integration as Google News, so you don't see the public profile of the writer of a piece.

YouTube (another Google service) isn't using +1 at the time I write this; it still has the old Like button, although I expect +1 to be integrated with YouTube at some point.

Integrating +1 with Your Website

If you run a website, then you might want to integrate +1 with your own pages. This is easy enough to do, and Google provides a web page that will generate the code for you at www.google.com/webmasters/+1/button.

This web page (shown in Figure 10-7) enables you to create a snippet of HTML code that you can embed in your web page.

FIGURE 10-7 Creating the code for a +1 button for a website.

- -

WHAT IF I RUN A BLOG? If you use one of the popular blogging platforms (such as WordPress or Blogger), then you'll find integration with +1 baked into the system. Check your dashboard preferences for sharing options.

- -

Follow these steps on Google's +1 code generator site to add a +1 button to your website:

1. **Choose a size.** This is the width of the button on the page. Four sizes are available: Small (15px), Standard (24px), Medium (20px) and Tall (60px).

2. **Select the annotation.** This relates to the information on how many people have +1'd your content. The annotation can be inline, bubble, or none. If you choose bubble or none, skip to step 4.

3. **Type the width.** If you choose inline annotation, you can choose the width of the annotation. The default is 450 pixels.

4. **Select the language.** The default is English (US), but you can choose the language most appropriate to your site.

5. **Click Advanced options.** The following advanced options are available:

   + **Asynchronous.** This option (selected by default) ensures that the buttons load independently of the page and reduces load time.

   + **HTML5 valid syntax.** This option (unselected by default) renders the script in the newer HTML5 syntax.

   + **Parse.** Two options are in the drop-down list: Default (On Load) and Explicit. Default (On Load) renders all buttons after the page loads, and Explicit renders the button at that point on the page.

   + **JS Callback function.** With this text box, advanced developers can implement a custom JavaScript function to take place when the +1 button is clicked.

   + **URL to +1.** You can specify a custom URL to go with the +1 button.

Below these Advanced options you'll find options for creating the customized snippet. They can be used to customize the content information passed on to Google:

   + **Page Type.** Choose the type of page (Blog, Article, Event, and so on) that most closely matches the page you'll use the snippet on.

   + **Title.** Add a title for the snippet.

   + **Image URL.** Add a URL to an image to go with the snippet.

   + **Description.** Add a description of the content you are sharing.

   + **Markup Location.** Two options for you to place the code are available: `<head>` and `<body>`. Choose the place you want to insert the code.

When you are done, you simply cut and paste the code produced in the text boxes to your website and +1 will be integrated.

WHAT IF THE CODE ISN'T UPDATING PROPERLY? You may need to refresh your browser for the code to update in the main display.

Managing Your +1 Web Content in Google+

After you have been using +1 for a while, you may want to start checking over, and perhaps removing, your +1 information in Google+.

You can look at your +1 information in your profile. Click your account icon and then click the +1's link in the gray menu strip above your Stream. All your +1 activity appears in the Stream. At the bottom of the list is a See more +1's link; click it to display more information.

ADDING +1 CONTENT TO YOUR PROFILE

It's great that Google keeps track of your +1 information, although you might not want everybody to see everything that you +1'd. Because of this, your +1 content isn't automatically listed for other people to view on Google+ (that's the difference between using +1 and the Share icon).

However, you might think that it's a great thing for other people to be able to check out your +1's (I certainly do). If so, you can show your +1 clicks as part of your profile. Follow these steps (as shown in Figure 10-8) to publicly display your +1's:

1. Click your account icon.
2. Click Edit Profile.
3. Click +1's in the profile menu bar.
4. Select the Show this tab on your profile check box.
5. Click Save.
6. Click Done Editing.

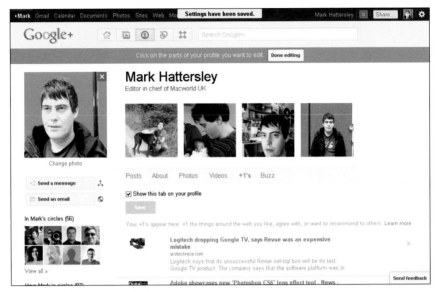

FIGURE 10-8 Your +1 activity.

You won't personally notice a difference, because you can view your +1's already, but the +1 tab will now appear on your profile when other people look at it. It's possible to test this out by clicking View Profile As and choosing Anyone on the web.

Of course, if you're going to have your +1 information publicly available, you might want to be careful which +1 items you click. It's far easier to click +1 than it is to share a post on Google+.

IS IT POSSIBLE TO LIMIT MY +1'S TO PEOPLE IN MY CIRCLES? No, it doesn't seem possible at the moment. You can either have them on your profile, or not. You can limit whether your profile is publicly visible in search, though. Chapter 2 has more information on setting up your profile.

REMOVING +1 CONTENT FROM YOUR PROFILE

As with posts, there may come a time when you decide to remove items you have +1'd from Google+ (either because you no longer feel it's appropriate or for general housecleaning).

Removing content you have +1'd is easy enough. There are two methods, and I mentioned the first method earlier in this chapter: Go to the website or post and click the +1 button again to deselect it. This removes your +1 from that web page as well as your +1 list in Google+.

Of course, visiting every web page again isn't always that easy or practical, so Google also enables you to remove +1 content using Google+. Do the following to remove +1's:

1. **Click your account icon.**

2. **Click +1's in the profile menu bar.**

3. **Click the X icon next to a +1 (as shown in Figure 10-9).**

The +1 is removed from the list on Google+ (and the original website, if you clicked it there). You can click Undo to restore the +1. It's not possible (at the moment) to delete all your +1's in one fell swoop; you have to manage each one individually.

WILL PEOPLE STILL BE ABLE TO SEE MY +1? Not on your profile page, but if you also shared the page as a post, it is not deleted along with the +1. You need to delete the post separately. Chapter 6 has more information on deleting posts.

FIGURE 10-9 Removing a +1 from your profile.

Related Questions

+ How do I edit my Google+ profile? **CHAPTER 2, Completing Your Google+ Profile**

+ How do I manage information I've posted to Google+? **CHAPTER 6, Managing Posts**

+ What is Google doing with +1 information? **CHAPTER 15, Discovering Just How Much Google Knows About You**

CHAPTER ELEVEN

HOW DO I PLAY GAMES ON GOOGLE+?

In this chapter:

+ Finding Games to Play
+ Installing Games
+ Spending Money on Games
+ Removing or Deleting Games

One of the great aspects of social networking sites is social gaming. These are games that you play through the web browser on your own or with friends.

It's the early days for gaming on Google+, and as I write, only 43 games are available. The good news is that they're pretty much the cream of the crop: Angry Birds, CityVille, Zynga Poker, Mafia Wars 2, and Edgeworld are all great ways to while away the hours. All the games on Google+ are free to play (although some do support in-game transactions, giving you extra features). Gaming in Google+ couldn't be easier. The games are listed on the All games page, and you can be up and running in a matter of minutes.

Finding Games to Play

To find games to play in Google+, click the games icon in the menu bar. By default this brings up a selection of featured games, as shown in Figure 11-1. The main screen displays a large graphic of a featured game and moves through a slide show of games (you can click any of the icons at the bottom to pick a game).

If any of your friends have played the game recently, their profile pictures also appear next to the Play button in the bottom-left of the screen.

FIGURE 11-1 Featured games.

In the left-hand column you also have the following options (as shown in Figure 11-2):

+ **Notifications.** Your game alerts (such as if you've received a gift or if a person has invited you to play a game with them) appear in this section.

+ **Recent games.** Games you have played recently appear here.

+ **Featured games.** The default option displays selected highlights divided into three categories: New games, Top games, and Staff picks.

+ **All games.** All the games available on Google+ are in this section.

Because only a few games are available at the moment, you can't look for games in the Google+ search box, although I imagine search functionality will be implemented at a later date, when the number of games on Google+ expands.

FIGURE 11-2 Locating different games.

Installing Games

In Google+, you don't really install games in a traditional sense, because they aren't stored on your computer; instead, you play them through your web browser using Adobe Flash. Click the blue Play button next to a game to start it (in the All games section you need to hover the mouse over a game icon for the Play button to appear, as shown in Figure 11-3).

You need to grant a game permission to run in Google+ for the first time. When you first run

FIGURE 11-3 Click the Play button.

a game, a request window appears (as shown in Figure 11-4). This shows the permissions that the game requests to play. Typically a game requests basic information about your account and permission to view people in your Circles based on your interaction with them.

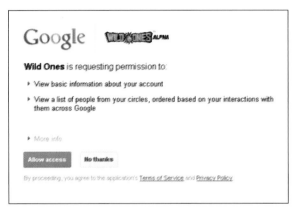

FIGURE 11-4 Games request permission to access your information.

Click Allow access to play the game or No thanks to deny that game access to your information. A lot of what games ask for is perfectly legitimate, such as information on who is playing the game and who your friends are so a game can form interactions between players. (On each level of Angry Birds you get to see which of your friends has the highest score, for example.)

But it's also true that games are being developed to give manufacturers your information for marketing. Typically, games use your information to provide interaction with people in your Circles. When Google rolls out ads (which I presume will happen), the information game developers collect will ensure you see ads based on the things you like. Take note that when you share your information with game developers, you're also sharing your email address with them. Chapter 15 has more information on Google+ and privacy issues.

CAN I ASK QUESTIONS BEFORE INSTALLATION? On installation click Learn more to reveal the email address of the developer so you can ask for more information on how your information is used. The developer can also provide general support.

Once you've allowed a game access, you are able to play it inside your browser. Each game works differently, but typically a game runs through an introduction to the basic controls before you start playing.

When you have installed a few games, you see a Games Stream appear below the slide show in the Featured games section (as shown in Figure 11-5). This shows the gaming activity of other people in your Circles. Typically you'll see any special achievements that they have shared with you. As with other posts, you can +1 this achievement, comment on it, or share it with your Circles. As you play games, you will often be asked if you want to post your achievements or score to Google+. If you and your friends are avid gamers, this is a great way to get bragging rights and start a chat about games.

FIGURE 11-5 The Games Stream.

WHAT IF A GAME DOESN'T WORK? Games in Google+ are created using Adobe Flash. If a game isn't running properly, you probably haven't got Adobe Flash installed correctly or aren't running the latest version. Go to www.adobe.com/products/flashplayer.html to install the latest update.

Spending Money on Games

Although all games are free to play and install in Google+, some of them enable you to exchange real-life money for virtual money to spend in the game. Each game does this differently, but each one works with Google's payment system: Google Checkout. I'm using Monster World as an example, but in most games (apart from the initial request to spend money) the purchase system is the same. Here is how you spend money in Monster World:

1. **Click the coin icon in the top-left of the screen.**

2. **Select the amount of coins you want.** If you don't have enough "monster cash" (which is what you earn in the game to exchange for coins), a window offering you the option to buy the coins appears.

3. **Click Add Monster Cash.**

4. **Choose an amount to spend (between $2.29 and $164.30 in this game) and click OK.**

5. **A Google account window opens.** Click Start now.

6. **A new window opens asking you to sign in with your Google account.** Type your password and click Sign in.

7. **Read the terms of service and select the I have read and accept these documents check box.**

8. **Click Sign up.**

9. **Review your purchase.** If you already have a Google account linked to a credit card, it appears in the window. Otherwise click the card details and choose Add a new payment method from the drop-down list.

10. **A Google Checkout window appears (as shown in Figure 11-6).** Type your location, card number, expiration date, name, street address, and phone number. All of this information is used for account verification.

11. **Click Add and continue.**

12. **Click Complete your purchase.**

13. **Click Close when the payment has gone through.**

Almost all games use payment as a shortcut for playing the game, so it is possible to get the same result simply by spending time playing the game (which is what I think the game is for in the first place — but lots of my friends have spent money on social games).

Add a new payment method

Google Checkout allows you to make payments using your Google Account.

Location	United States (US)
Card number	VISA AMEX DISCOVER
Expiration date	Month Year CVC
Name	
Street address	
City	
State	Alabama
Zip code	
Phone	

Required for account verification

Add and continue   Cancel

FIGURE 11-6 Adding your credit card information to Google Checkout.

- -

HOW CAN I EDIT MY GOOGLE CHECKOUT INFORMATION? You can't edit Google Checkout information in Google+. Instead type **checkout. google.com** into your browser to edit your shipping address or payment methods and view your purchase history.

- -

Removing or Deleting Games

There may come a point when you no longer want to play a game anymore. Unlike most video games, the games on Google+ do not take up space on your system, and if you're no longer using them, they won't post to your Stream or share information with your Circles.

What I'm saying is that you don't really need to uninstall games from Google+ in the traditional sense. As with all apps, you can simply stop using them.

Having said that, some people prefer to remove unwanted games from their Google+ account to prevent the developer from having access to their personal data. You can do this by removing permissions for a game:

1. **Start the game you'd like to remove permissions for.**

2. **Click the gear icon to the right of the main game window and choose Remove game (as shown in Figure 11-7).**

3. **A list pop-up confirmation window appears.** This informs you that removing the game revokes the permissions you have granted to the developer and

FIGURE 11-7 The Remove game option.

removes the game from your list. Click Okay, got it to remove the game (as shown in Figure 11-8).

The game is removed from your list of Recent games. To play the game again you will need to click Play, and load the game again.

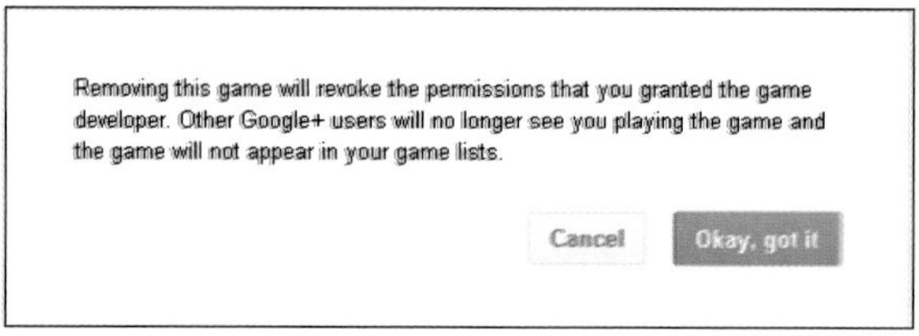

Removing this game will revoke the permissions that you granted the game developer. Other Google+ users will no longer see you playing the game and the game will not appear in your game lists.

Cancel   Okay, got it

FIGURE 11-8 Revoking a game's permissions and removing it from your game list.

Related Questions

+ How do I share my gaming information with people? **CHAPTER 5, Getting to Know Circles**

+ How do I manage my privacy with Google? **CHAPTER 15, Using the Google+ Profile and Privacy Settings**

HOW DO I MANAGE GOOGLE+ SETTINGS?

Google+ is a much more detailed web service than you'd imagine. Beneath the shiny web-based hood is a powerful engine of interrelated and interconnected services designed to hook you up to the world.

As with any complicated machine, there's a large amount of tweaking and testing you can do to customize Google+ with your own preferences. Becoming familiar with the settings is a great idea if you want to get the most of Google+.

Accessing the Google Accounts Settings

Google+ has an integrated settings page known as Google accounts, which you can access via the Google+ bar. Click your account icon (the small thumbnail image of your profile) in the Google+ bar to reveal the account settings, as shown in Figure 12-1. This reveals Account settings and Privacy. Clicking either of these takes you to the Google accounts page. The other two options (Profile and Google+) link back to areas on the Google+ site.

FIGURE 12-1 Accessing Profile or Account settings.

The following options appear in the left-hand column of the Google accounts page (as shown in Figure 12-2):

+ Account overview

+ Profile and privacy

+ Google+

+ Language

+ Data liberation

+ Connected accounts

You learn about the options available in each of these areas in this chapter. When you're finished editing settings, return to Google+ by clicking +*Yourname* icon in the Google+ bar (or clicking the account icon and choosing Profile).

FIGURE 12-2 The Google accounts page displaying Google+ settings.

Looking at the Account Overview

The Account overview settings enable you to access and change your password (and other security options) and email addresses, and delete parts of your account.

CHANGING YOUR PASSWORD

Click Change password if you want to choose a new security login. A new screen appears that enables you to choose a new password. Follow these steps:

1. **Type your current password.** Alternatively, type the secret word you choose when signing up for a Google account. You can see a hint for the word next to the text box.

2. **Type the new password in the two text boxes below.** Both boxes need to have the same text and a Password strength meter indicates how secure the password is.

3. **Click Save.**

You remain logged in to Google+, but next time you log in, you need to use the new password.

CHANGING RECOVERY OPTIONS

Google provides a recovery system in case you forget your password and login details. By default this is a second email address or a hint to a secret word that only you know, and you set these up during the Google+ sign-up process. Chapter 1 has more information on signing up for Google+.

However, you can add or change the email address, choose a new secret word, or add a cell phone number at any point (as shown in Figure 12-3).

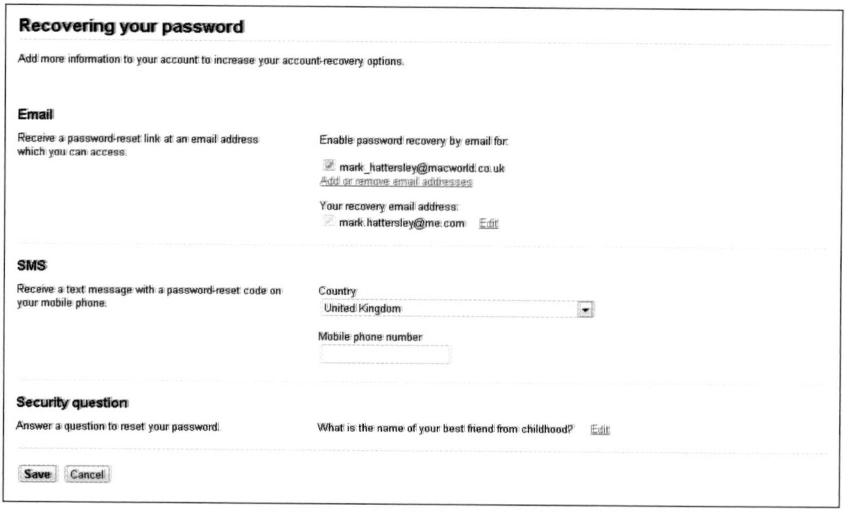

FIGURE 12-3 Changing your recovery options on the Google accounts page.

Click Change recovery options. You may need to reenter your password, and then click OK to see the options available:

+ **Email.** You can add additional email addresses to recover your email by clicking Add or remove email addresses, or click Edit to change your default recovery email address.

+ **SMS.** You can sign up to receive a text message on your mobile phone (you can enter this into Google+ to reset your Google+ account). Do the following to add a number to Google+:

1. Click **Add a mobile phone number**.

2. Choose a country from the drop-down list.

3. Type your cell phone number into the **Mobile phone number** text box.

4. Click **Save**.

5. You may be asked to type your password before you click **Verify**.

+ **Security question.** Click Edit and choose an option from the Question drop-down list, write your response in the Answer text box, and click Save.

I think it's a pretty good idea to add your cell phone number to Google as a form of password recovery. It saves a lot of hassle with answering detailed security questions if you ever try to recover your account. But don't forget to update the number if you get a new phone.

ACTIVATING MULTIPLE SIGN-IN

It is possible to sign in to Google with different accounts and switch between them. The Account overview page enables you to activate and deactivate multiple sign-in. Note that this affects not just Google+ but also a set of other Google products, including Calendar, Gmail, and News. As you activate it, the warning message shown in Figure 12-4 appears.

FIGURE 12-4 Controlling multiple sign-in.

HOW DO I SIGN IN USING A DIFFERENT ACCOUNT?

If more than one person uses Google+ on the same computer, it is possible to set up the service so multiple people can sign in and out on the same web browser. Do the following to sign in with multiple accounts:

1. **Click the account icon in the Google+ bar and click Switch account.**

2. **Click Sign in to another account.**

3. **Type your email address and password and click Sign in.**

Now you are able to switch between accounts by clicking your account icon, clicking Switch account, and choosing the required account from the list.

You can sign out of the account by clicking your account icon and then clicking Sign out, or sign out of all open accounts by clicking the account icon, clicking Switch account, and then clicking Sign out of all accounts.

Two options are available:

+ **On.** You can use multiple Google accounts in the same web browser. This has three check boxes that you need to select before you can save the changes.

+ **Off.** You can only use one account at a time.

If this is the first time you are using multiple sign-in, you should read the notes and select each box. From then on, the decision is saved. Click Save to commit to the changes.

SETTING UP 2-STEP VERIFICATION

If you often use Google+ from different computers, you can set up an extra security system called *2-step verification* that works in conjunction with your cell phone (in a similar fashion to password recovery).

With this system switched on, you'll receive a code on your cell phone when using a computer that's different from one you normally use. This prevents strangers (who may have cracked, or guessed, your password) from accessing your account. To do this, you need to enter your cell phone number into Google+ and enter a code that Google sends via text to your cell phone (as shown in Figure 12-5).

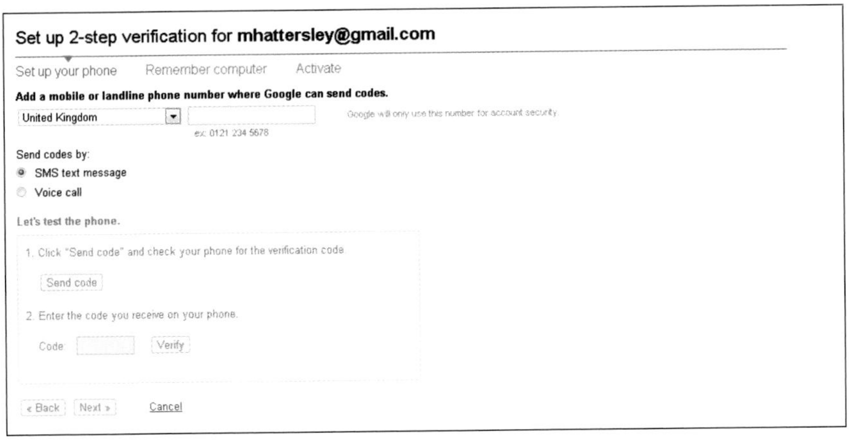

Set up 2-step verification for **mhattersley@gmail.com**

Set up your phone   Remember computer   Activate

Add a mobile or landline phone number where Google can send codes.

United Kingdom | ▼ | | | Google will only use this number for account security.

ex: 0121 234 5678

Send codes by:
● SMS text message
○ Voice call

Let's test the phone.

1. Click "Send code" and check your phone for the verification code.

Send code

2. Enter the code you receive on your phone.

Code: | Verify

‹ Back | Next › | Cancel

FIGURE 12-5 Setting up 2-step verification.

Follow these steps to set up 2-step verification:

1. **Click 2-step verification on the Google Account overview page.**

2. **Click Start setup.**

3. **Choose your country from the drop-down list and add your mobile phone number.**

4. **By default, codes are sent by SMS text message, so click Voice call if you'd prefer Google's automated voice service to call you and read out the number.**

5. **Click Send code to receive a test code.**

6. **Check your cell phone for the code.** When it arrives, type it into the Code text box and click Verify.

7. **When the test code has been verified, click Next.**

8. **If you are using a public computer (or one you don't normally use) you should deselect the Remember this computer for 30 days check box.**

9. **Click Next.**

10. **Click Turn on 2-step verification.**

11. **A warning message appears stating that some third-party apps and mobile devices may not work until you create new passwords (as shown in Figure 12-6).** Click Do this later.

A great thing about 2-step verification is that it provides your Google+ account with fairly comprehensive protection from intruders (since they need to have your mobile phone to access your account).

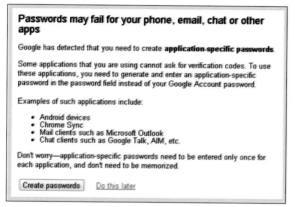

Passwords may fail for your phone, email, chat or other apps

Google has detected that you need to create **application-specific passwords**.

Some applications that you are using cannot ask for verification codes. To use these applications, you need to generate and enter an application-specific password in the password field instead of your Google Account password.

Examples of such applications include:

- Android devices
- Chrome Sync
- Mail clients such as Microsoft Outlook
- Chat clients such as Google Talk, AIM, etc.

Don't worry—application-specific passwords need to be entered only once for each application, and don't need to be memorized.

[Create passwords]   Do this later

FIGURE 12-6 2-step verification warning that apps may not work.

The downside of this is that you need to authorize every different computer that you use, and the extra step involving your mobile phone can be a pain. And you need to have your mobile phone in hand, it must be charged, and it must have network coverage, which might not be the case if you're overseas and using a temporary computer (although Google does have a work-around that involves temporary codes, covered later in this chapter).

More important, some applications on your computer (such as Windows Live Mail and Outlook) stop working until you authorize them. This also applies to apps on your mobile phone. So you may need to create special passwords for these apps. You can do this using the Google website or the Google Authenticator app on a mobile phone.

Using the Google Authenticator app to receive codes

If you don't have cell coverage, you can use the Google Authenticator app on Android, iPhone, or BlackBerry to receive 2-step verification codes. You can use these when you have a Wi-Fi connection but no cell coverage (which is often the case when you're overseas).

Follow these steps to set up your mobile application to receive codes on an Android mobile device or iPhone (the BlackBerry app works slightly differently, so I explain that next):

1. **Go to the Account overview page and click Edit next to 2-step verification.**

2. **Click Android or iPhone, depending on your phone type.**

3. **Go to Google Play or the App Store and search for Google Authenticator.**

4. **Install and open the app.** On Android you may also be requested to install a QR barcode scanning app such as ZXing.

5. **Tap Scan a barcode in the Google Authenticator app (on an iPhone you need to tap the + icon first).**

6. **Use the mobile phone's camera to scan the QR barcode that is displayed on the screen (as shown in Figure 12-7).**

7. **Type the six-digit number displayed on the Google Authenticator app in the Code text box and click Verify.**

8. **Click Save.**

In many ways, using the Google Authenticator app to authorize a new computer is faster and easier than getting a message sent to your cell phone. So it's well worth the time to install Google Authenticator. The Google Authenticator app works in conjunction with other apps installed on the phone to provide instant 2-step authorization. (If the developer has provided support, the app itself requests a code be sent to the Google Authenticator app on your phone; you only need to open Google Authenticator to view the code.)

FIGURE 12-7 Scan this QR barcode using Google Authenticator to set up a mobile phone.

If you have a BlackBerry, the process of setting up 2-step verification to receive codes on the phone is slightly different:

1. Go to m.google.com/authenticator on your BlackBerry browser and click Download to get the Google Authenticator app.

2. Choose Yes to Trusted application status and click Select on your BlackBerry, and then click OK.

3. Go to the Account overview page in Google+ on your computer and click Edit next to 2-step verification.

4. Click BlackBerry next to Mobile Application.

5. Open the Google Authenticator app on the BlackBerry phone and choose Manual key entry.

6. Type the full email address associated with your Google account into the Account name box.

7. Type the Secret key code displayed in Google+ into the Enter key box (you don't need to worry about the spaces). If you enter

any incorrect letters or numbers, the BlackBerry displays the message Invalid key format.

8. **Ensure that the Type of key menu displays Time based and click Save.**

9. **Google Authenticator displays a six-digit number.** Type this into the Code box in the Google accounts page and click Verify.

10. **Click Save.** You are now able to use your BlackBerry to receive access codes to authorize remote computers.

Printing backup codes

If you are traveling and don't have access to your phone, you can use backup codes to access your Google+ account. You can print these out, and each code enables you to sign in to Google once.

1. **Go to the Account overview page and click Edit next to 2-step verification.** You may need to reenter your password.

2. **Click Show/Generate codes (next to Printable backup codes).** A set of ten codes appears (as shown in Figure 12-8).

3. **Click Print codes.**

4. **Click Print.**

Alternatively, you can choose Save to text file instead of printing them, although you should have a printed copy of the codes if you're going to be without your own laptop and cell phone.

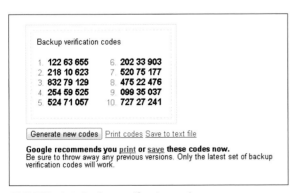

FIGURE 12-8 Backup verification codes.

HOW LONG DO VERIFICATION CODES LAST? Codes only work once and only one set of codes works at any time. You can get a new set of codes by clicking Generate new codes, but the previous set will no longer work.

Entering a 2-Step verification code

When you get a new computer, you need to enter the 2-step verification code to be able to access your account.

After logging in to Google+, enter a verification code (as shown in Figure 12-9). If you have set up Google Authenticator on your mobile phone, open the app to receive the code. Otherwise it is delivered via SMS or a voice call (depending on which option you choose upon setting up 2-step delivery).

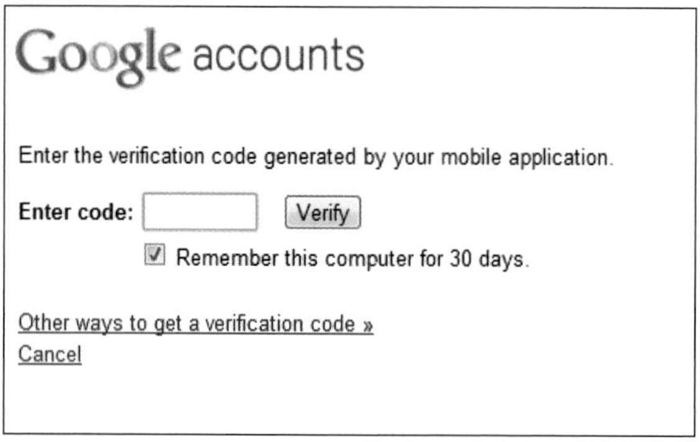

FIGURE 12-9 Entering a 2-step verification code.

If you do not have your mobile phone or wish to receive a code any other way, click Other ways to get a verification code and choose from one of the following:

+ Send to your backup phone number ending in *XXXX*, where *XXXX* is the last four digits of your phone number.

+ Use a backup code

+ I no longer have access to any of these

Enter the six-digit number into the Enter code text box and click Verify.

RECOVERING YOUR ACCOUNT

If you click I no longer have access to any of these on the 2-step verification page, you are taken to a Password Help screen to recover your account (this is a unique page for 2-step verification users who no longer have access to the mobile device associated with the account or any backup codes). This is handy if you switch phone numbers without updating 2-step verification and suddenly find yourself trying to access your account while away from your computer.

You need to enter a lot of detailed information regarding your Google account, including your old phone numbers associated with the account, estimates of when you first signed up and last logged in, frequently emailed contacts, and Gmail labels. You don't need to know all of this information, but if you enter enough of the information as accurately possible, Gmail should enable you to log in to your site.

AUTHORIZING APPLICATIONS AND SITES

If you decide that you want to combine the added security of having 2-step verification, you will discover that some of your computer programs and phone apps (such as Windows Live Mail, Google Picasa desktop app, and mobile Gmail) no longer work.

This is because they do not support 2-step verification, so you cannot enter the code that Google provides on your phone. Instead, you need to generate a specific password for each application. Follow these steps to authorize Windows Live Mail after you've turned on 2-step verification:

1. **Go to the Account overview page and click Edit next to Authorizing applications & sites.** You may need to reenter your password.

2. **Scroll down to Application-specific passwords and enter a reference name for the app in the Name text box.** This doesn't have to be exact; it's just for your reference.

3. **Click Generate password.**

4. **The password appears inside a yellow box in the browser (as shown in Figure 12-10).** Highlight it, right-click, and choose Copy

(or write it down). Note that you can only access the code this one instance, so you should type it into the app immediately.

FIGURE 12-10 The application-specific password.

5. **Open the application that you want to use the code in (if you have already signed up for Google services, you receive an error message).** Locate the preference in that application where you need to enter your password.

6. **Enter the password generated in Step 4 instead of your usual Gmail password and click OK (as shown in Figure 12-11).**

FIGURE 12-11 Typing the password into the application.

You need to do this for each application and phone app that accesses Google services, which can be quite time consuming. But you only need to do it once (or at least once for each program or app), and it does offer a high level of security.

EDITING PERSONAL INFORMATION, EMAIL ADDRESSES, AND USERNAMES

By default, Google has two email addresses for you: the one you use to sign in to Google+ and a backup.

You can edit these email addresses (or add additional addresses) as well as change your personal information by clicking Edit next to Email addresses. This brings up a screen (shown in Figure 12-12) with the following options:

+ First name

+ Last name

+ Nickname

+ Zip code

+ Country

+ Time zone

+ Add an additional email address

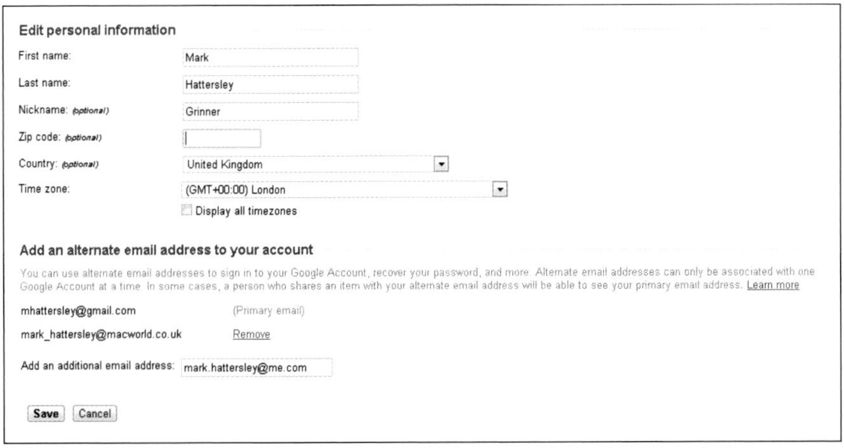

FIGURE 12-12 Editing personal information and adding email addresses.

Enter any additional information and click Save to enter the details into Google. You can also remove an email address by clicking Remove.

SERVICES

Three final options appear in the Account overview page under the Services heading:

+ Delete profile and Google+ features

+ Delete entire Google account

+ View, enable, or disable web history

As the names suggest, these options are used to delete your Google+ account or entire Google account as well as manage how Google uses your web search history. Chapter 15 has more detailed information on how to use these features to manage your privacy and delete your account.

Managing Profile and Privacy Settings

With so much of your personal information being stored online, you'd be wise to take a look at the profile and privacy settings. Click Profile and privacy in the left-hand column to see the following options:

+ **Search results.** This is the part of your Google+ profile that appears in Google Search results when somebody searches for you online. The image to the right displays how your profile looks in Google Search (as shown in Figure 12-13).

+ **Public profile information.** You can edit what information is displayed on your public profile. Click Edit visibility on profile to go to your profile page in Edit mode. Chapter 2 has more information on setting up your Google+ profile.

+ **See how your profile appears to other users**. Type a name of a person in your Circles into the Enter a username text box and click Preview to see how your profile appears to that person.

+ **Circles.** Click Manage circles to go to the Circles page. Chapter 5 has more information on managing Circles.

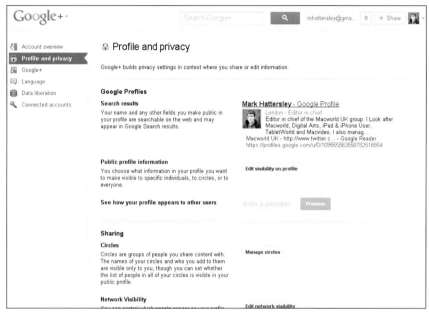

FIGURE 12-13 The profile and privacy settings.

+ **Network Visibility.** Click Edit network visibility. This opens the profile page in edit mode at the point where you can manage the parts of your Circles that are visible to other users.

+ **Who can share posts with you.** Click View incoming posts to look at the Incoming Stream.

+ **Who posts are shared with.** This outlines information on who posts information. You cannot adjust anything here; it merely explains the process for sharing posts with different Circles. Chapter 6 has more information on sharing posts with different Circles of people.

+ **Photos.** Click Edit photos settings to go to the Photos section in the Google+ settings.

+ **Hangouts.** This provides information on what happens when you start or join a Hangout. Nothing is editable in this section.

+ **Dashboard.** Click Sign into dashboard to view and manage information stored in your Google account.

+ **Privacy Center.** Click Go to Privacy Center for more information on Google's products and privacy policies.

Although Google information on privacy is comprehensive, it is scattered in many different locations, and managing it effectively can be difficult. Chapter 15 has information on managing privacy in Google+ effectively.

Fine-tuning Google+ Settings

The Google+ settings page offers a range of options that relate specifically to Google+ (rather than applying to Google as a whole). Click Google+ in the left-hand column of the Google accounts page to find the following options:

+ **Who can send you notifications?** Notifications are great because they let you know when people have shared or commented on your posts, mentioned you in a post, invited you to a game, invited you to a Hangout, or tagged you in a photo. If you have a lot of people in your Circles, though, you might find yourself getting too many notifications. You can choose who sends you notifications from the following options:

  + **Anyone**
  + **Extended circles**
  + **Your circles**
  + **Only you**
  + **Custom** (This enables you to choose specific people and Circles.)

+ **Who can start a Messenger conversation with you?** This controls who can start a message with you. The following options are available:

  + **Anyone**
  + **Extended circles**
  + **Circles**

+ **Set delivery preferences.** Here you can determine how Google+ can contact you. The following two options are available:

  + **Email.** This is not editable here. Instead it is edited using the Account overview settings, which are explained earlier in this chapter.

+ **Phone.** You can add a phone number here and Google notifies you via your mobile phone. Chapter 13 has more information on setting up and using Google+ on a mobile phone.

+ **Manage email subscriptions.** This check box (selected by default) allows Google to send you emails about Google+ activity and suggestions of new friends.

+ **Receive notifications.** You can choose to get notifications by email and SMS (mobile phone text message) using the check boxes shown in Figure 12-14.

+ **+1 on non-Google sites.** This enables you to choose whether Google can use your +1 information on other websites. When you click +1 on a post to a website page in Google+, other people see you when they hover over +1 on that website. This is enabled by default, but you can click Edit and choose Disable to disable it.

+ **Automatically add a Google+ page to my circles if I search for + followed by the page's name.** This option (unselected by default) enables you to add a page to Circles if you search for it.

+ **Show photo geo location information in newly uploaded albums and photos.** This option is disabled by default. If you want to upload geo location information captured with your photograph, select this check box.

+ **Allow viewers to download my photos.** This option is enabled by default. If you don't want users downloading your photos, deselect the check box.

+ **People whose tags of you are automatically approved to link to your profile.** The Your circles option is enabled by default. You can choose different groups of people who are authorized to tag you in photographs with this option.

When you've finished adjusting the Google+ settings, click Back to Google+ to move back to the home page.

FIGURE 12-14 The Receive notifications settings.

Adjusting the Language Settings

The Language page (as shown in Figure 12-15) is the most basic page in Google accounts. It has only two settings:

+ **Primary language.** This drop-down list enables you to choose the language that is used for the text throughout Google. Choose a different language and click Reload.

+ **Add Another Language.** This setting enables you to add a second language to the list of default languages. Then click Make primary to make that the default language. This makes it easier to switch between two commonly used languages.

- -

DO THE LANGUAGE SETTINGS WORK GLOBALLY? The language settings only affect Google+. Services such as Gmail, Calendar, and Google Search remain in the language associated with the website you are using (Google.co.fr will still be in French, for example).

- -

FIGURE 12-15 Changing the primary language.

Accessing Data Liberation

Google makes it easy for you to download data (including images, posts, and your Circles and contacts). You can easily get hold of this data thanks to a service called *Google Takeout*.

Follow these steps to get hold of your data:

1. **On the Data liberation page, click Download your data.**
2. **You may need to reenter your password.**
3. **Click Create Archive (as shown in Figure 12-16).** Loading bars appear on the screen while Google prepares the data for download.
4. **Click Download.** You may need to reenter your password.
5. **Click OK.**

The data is saved into your web browser's default Downloads folder as a zip file. When you unzip the file, it contains a series of folders containing the relevant documents. The Stream, Buzz, and Circles information are in HTML files, images are saved as JPEGs, and contacts are saved as VCF files.

You can also choose to download data from a specific service. Either click one of the listed services in Data liberation or click Choose services in Google Takeout, select a service (or several services), and click Create Archive (as shown in Figure 12-17).

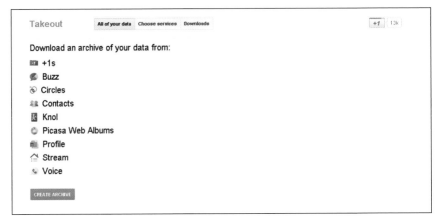

FIGURE 12-16 Access your data from Google.

FIGURE 12-17 Downloading data from a specific service.

Setting Up Connected Accounts

You have the option to hook up other social media services to Google using the Connected accounts. Google points out three advantages:

+ When you search, you can see relevant content your friends have shared on the web.

+ You make it easier for Google to find the stuff you share on the web and connect it to you in its search products.

+ You can choose which accounts to show on your public Google profile.

Google won't share the things you've searched for in Google without your consent. But even so, you might want to be careful when connecting too much of your personal social media to your Google account. While it makes it easier for people to find you, it also makes it much easier for them to learn a lot of information about you.

This is the example Google provides (on its Inside Search pages):

> Bob, whose Gmail address is surferguybob@gmail.com, is signed in to Google and searches for **california surf spots.** He may see a surfing web page shared by his friend Alice on Twitter, as well as a message asking him if he wants to connect his Twitter account, surferguybob, to his Google account. If he confirms, twitter.com/surferguybob will be connected to his Google account, allowing Bob to see more search results from the people he publicly follows on Twitter in the future.

Follow these steps to connect an account to Google:

1. **In the Google accounts page, click Connected accounts.**

2. **Click Connect an Account and choose a social media service (such as Facebook) from the drop-down list.**

3. **Enter an account name or link to your page on the social media service (as shown in Figure 12-18).** In most instances, you need to enter a specific URL, not just an account name.

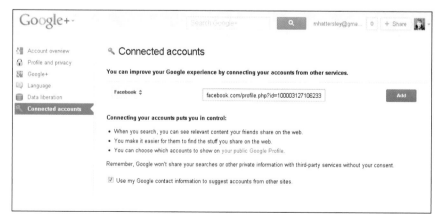

FIGURE 12-18 Connecting your Facebook account to your Google+ account.

4. **Click Add.**

5. **If you want the service to appear on your public profile, select the Show on my public Google profile check box.**

If you decide to disconnect a social media service from the site, click Remove next to the social service in the list of connected accounts.

You can currently add the following services to Google using this system:

+ Facebook

+ Yahoo!

+ Flickr

+ LinkedIn

+ Quora

+ Twitter

+ Yelp

+ Hotmail

+ Myspace

+ Plaxo

+ Last.fm

There is also a check box called Use my Google contact information to suggest accounts from other sites, which is selected by default. This option can help widen your social connections, and helps Google improve its search results. But if you'd rather Google not use your contact information to suggest other accounts to other people, deselect the box.

Related Questions

+ How do I choose a good password? **CHAPTER 1, Signing Up for Google+**

+ How do I use Google+ on my cell phone? **CHAPTER 13, Using the Google+ Mobile Website**

+ How much should I worry about Google and privacy? **CHAPTER 15, Discovering Just How Much Google Knows About You**

HOW DO I USE GOOGLE+ ON A MOBILE DEVICE?

I n recent years, computers have become increasingly mobile. Cell phones have evolved into smartphones, capable of full Internet access and armed with a range of lightweight programs (called *apps*) that place the functionality of desktop computing in the palm of your hand. And tablet devices, such as the Motorola Xoom and Apple iPad, provide a portable computing experience on par with a laptop, but with the persistent data connection of a smartphone.

This mobile computer boom has walked hand in hand with the rise in social media. People can now communicate from anywhere; they're not limited to only viewing the online world from inside their homes.

Smartphones have GPS and built-in cameras for photos and videos. And because you almost always carry a smartphone, you can send a steady stream of information about yourself to your social media contacts.

Using the Google+ Mobile Website

The first step when using Google+ on a smartphone is to look at the Google+ website (http://plus.google.com). If you access it from a mobile device, you see a mobile-optimized version of the Google+ site. To access the site, you need to fill in the Email and Password text boxes and tap Sign in. This takes you to the mobile website (as shown in Figure 13-1).

The Google+ mobile website offers much of the functionality of the main website, plus a few extra features. The majority of the display is the Stream, and you can scroll up and down new posts from people you are following.

The Google+ menu bar has four icons:

FIGURE 13-1 The Google+ mobile website.

+ **Home.** This icon is displayed on nearly every screen. Tap it to return to the main page.

+ **Refresh.** Tap this icon to view new posts in the Stream.

+ **Check mark.** Tap this icon to check into your location.

+ **Post.** Tap the post (pencil) icon to share your thoughts.

Below these icons are three options that you can use to view different types of Streams:

+ **Circles.** People who are in your Circles.

+ **Incoming.** People who are following you.

+ **Nearby.** People who are near your physical location (as determined by the phone's location services).

You can choose between these three different Streams by swiping left and right across the
Stream in the main display.

A right-facing arrow appears next to each
post in the Stream. Tapping it opens the post in
its own window (as shown in Figure 13-2). Here
are some of the things you can do with a post:

+ **Tap +1.** This +1's the post.

+ **Tap the down-arrow icon.** This gives you
the option to share a post (you can also
report abuse and mute a post from this
menu).

+ **Tap a link in a post to open it in a new
window in the mobile browser.**

FIGURE 13-2 Looking at a
post in the mobile browser.

+ **Tap a person's name to view details.**

+ **Tap an image to open it in a photo viewer.**

+ **Tap in the Comment text box to enter a response.** Then tap Post to
send it.

CHECKING INTO LOCATIONS

One neat thing about the Google+ mobile website is that it integrates with
a smartphone's location services to check you into a location (to let people
know where you are). This is a key feature that you are more likely to use on

a smartphone than on a laptop, even if you are working in a mobile fashion. Here's how to check into your location:

1. **Tap the check mark icon in the Stream.**

2. **If this is the first time you are using location services, you need to approve it by selecting the Remember preference check box and tapping Share location.** A list of the nearby locations Google recognizes appears (as shown in Figure 13-3).

3. **If the location is in the list, tap it to check in and add it to your post (as shown in Figure 13-4).**

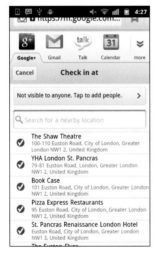

FIGURE 13-3 A list of locations you can check into.

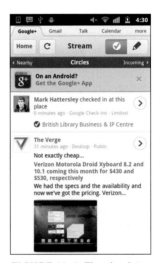

FIGURE 13-4 The check-in as it appears on your post.

HOW DOES MY PHONE KNOW WHERE I AM? Mobile phones use a combination of GPS satellites, and Wi-Fi hotspot and cellular data tower triangulation to determine your position. Because GPS provides the most accurate location, services are more accurate when you're outdoors.

You can also search for a nearby location by typing its name into the search text box. Typically, bars, shops, restaurants, and landmarks are included in Google's database of locations.

CAN I VIEW LOCATIONS ON A MAP? If a person has shared his or her location on a post, the address appears. Press the Menu button when viewing a post and tap Map to open it in Google Maps.

CREATING A POST

Using the mobile version of Google+, you can post on the go. Follow these steps to quickly share your thoughts while you're on the move:

1. **In the Google+ app, tap the post (pencil) icon.**

2. **Tap the center of the screen to bring up the keyboard.**

3. **Type your post into the text box (as shown in Figure 13-5).** Tap outside of the text box to bring back the controls.

4. **Use the Circles text box to select the Circles or individuals you want to add.** Tap Done or OK.

5. **Tap the + icon next to No location attached to add your location information.** Google tries to guess the nearest location, but if you tap a listed location, you can choose from the list.

FIGURE 13-5 Creating a post.

6. **Tap the post icon to add the text to your Stream.**

   The great thing about the Google+ mobile website is that you can quickly share a thought online, no matter where you are. The downside is that you are limited to sharing text and location; you can't share anything more complicated, such as photos and videos. For that sort of functionality, you need to install the Google+ app (which I cover later in this chapter).

USING OTHER GOOGLE+ FEATURES ONLINE

By default the Google+ mobile website takes you to the Stream, so you might find it easy to overlook the other features the website offers. You can access them by tapping Home. The following are available:

+ **Stream.** The default landing page that shows recent posts.

+ **Photos.** Tap this icon to view photos from your Circles, pictures in which you are tagged, and your albums. You can't upload photos to Google+ from the mobile website, however.

+ **Circles.** Tap this icon to view all the different people in your Circles. You can only view Circles and the individuals within them. You cannot create or manage Circles.

+ **Profile.** Tap this icon this to view your profile (as shown in Figure 13-6). You can view the About, Posts, and Photos pages.

+ **Notifications.** Tap this icon to view notifications regarding activity on your Google+ account.

FIGURE 13-6   A profile on the Google+ mobile website.

I like the Google+ mobile website because it offers quick access to Google+ and (for a website) is packed with a lot of functionality. But there's no doubt in my mind that you should take the time to install the Google+ app if you have an Android- or iOS-based mobile device (Apple iPhone or iPod touch). The app packs a lot more power and offers a wider range of functions, as well as a slicker interface.

CAN I ADD PEOPLE TO CIRCLES?   Yes, but not through the Circles page. If you tap a person's name in the Stream, you see an Add to circles option.

Installing the Google+ App

Google has created a custom app of Google+ for both Android and iOS users. You can download the versions from Google Play (formerly called the Android Market) and the Apple App Store for iOS users.

Aside from a few interface changes, the Google+ app is largely the same on Android and iOS devices. However, because Android and Google+ are Google products, the Android version tends to have a few extra features (such as Instant Upload for photos) and is usually updated with new features first. Both iOS and Android smartphone owners get a vastly improved Google+ experience by installing the Google+ app, so I recommend downloading it as soon as possible.

INSTALLING THE GOOGLE+ APP ON ANDROID

Follow these steps to download and install the Google+ app from Google Play (formerly called the Android Market):

1. **Tap the apps icon and tap Market.** If this is the first time you've used Google Play, you need to click Accept to accept the terms and conditions.

2. **Tap the Search icon in the top-right of the screen.**

3. **Type** Google+ **into the Search Google Play text box.**

4. **Tap Google+ from the list of apps (it should be top of the list).** A description of the app appears in the main window (as shown in Figure 13-7).

5. **Tap Free and OK to start the download.** The app is downloaded in the background. Wait for a message that the item has downloaded to appear in the notifications bar at the top of the screen.

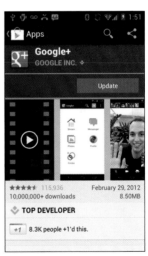

FIGURE 13-7 The Google+ app in Google Play.

6. Tap the Home button to return to the Home window.

7. Tap apps and then tap Google+.

8. **The email address associated with your Android phone should appear in the list, and if it is the same as your Google+ account, tap it.** Otherwise tap Create a New Account and type your Google+ email address and password.

9. **When you first open Google+, you are asked if you want to Enable Instant Upload, and you need to choose one of three options.** Chapter 8 has more information on using Instant Upload with photographs. The options include:

   + Over Wi-Fi or mobile network.

   + Over Wi-Fi only.

   + Disable Instant Upload.

10. **Choose the appropriate option (I normally choose Over Wi-Fi only) and tap Continue.** This takes you to the main window of the Google+ app, which has five icons for the main areas of Google+: Stream, Messenger, Photos, Profile, and Circles.

INSTALLING THE GOOGLE+ APP ON AN iOS DEVICE

Follow these steps to install the Google+ app on your iPhone or iPod touch:

FIGURE 13-8 The Google+ app in the App Store.

1. **Tap App Store.**

2. **Tap Search and type** Google+ **into the search text box.**

3. **Tap Google+ from the list of Search results.**

4. **Tap Free and then tap Install (as shown in Figure 13-8).**

5. **Type your Apple ID password and tap OK.** The app installs.

6. **Tap the Google+ app icon and tap Get started and Sign In.**

7. **Enter the email and password associated with your Google account.** Tap Sign In to go to the app's home screen.

8. **A pop-up message appears saying Google+ would like to send you push notifications.** Tap OK if you want the iOS device to notify you about activity on your account, or tap Don't Allow.

The home screen of the Google+ iPhone app has five main areas: Stream, Messenger, Photos, Profile, and Circles. Tap these icons to start using the Google+ app.

- -

IS THERE A BLACKBERRY VERSION? Google is only making versions for iOS and Android devices for the time being. BlackBerry users can continue to use the mobile website, though.

- -

Getting Started with the Google+ App

The Google+ app is largely the same on Android and iOS devices (as shown in Figure 13-9 and Figure 13-10). It has a similar interface and elements, although some elements are in different locations.

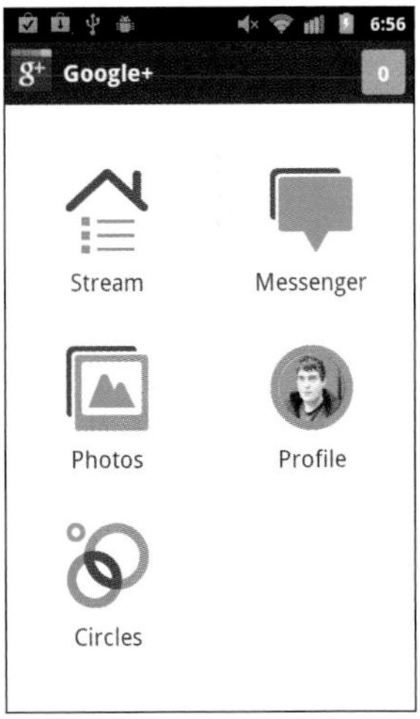

The following elements appear in the center of the screen and are common to both applications:

+ Stream

+ Messenger

+ Photos

+ Profile

+ Circles

Notifications appear in a gray box at the top-right of the Android app and at the bottom of the display on the iOS version. Tapping a notification item opens the list of recent activity.

FIGURE 13-9 The Google+ app on Android.

On the Android version, pressing the phone's Menu button gives you the following options (as shown in Figure 13-11):

+ Settings

+ Send feedback

+ Sign out

+ Help

+ Privacy policy

+ Terms of service

Another key difference is that in the iOS version, shortcut icons for Messenger and Post appear at the top-right of the screen. The iOS version also has a search box. Tap it to search for posts and people in Google+.

FIGURE 13-10 The Google+ app on iOS.

ADJUSTING SETTINGS ON THE ANDROID APP

FIGURE 13-11 Menu options on the Android app.

To access the Settings on the Google+ app for Android, press the Menu button and tap Settings. The Settings menu (as shown in Figure 13-12) has the following options.

Google+ notifications

+ **Google+ notifications.** Enabled by default and determines whether notifications relating to Google+ activity appear in the status bar.

+ **Vibrate.** Determines whether the mobile device vibrates when new notifications are received.

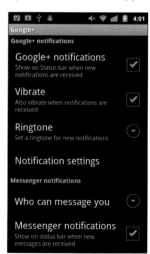

FIGURE 13-12 Settings on the Google+ Android app.

+ **Ringtone.** Enables you to choose a custom ringtone for new Google+ notifications.

+ **Notification settings.** Determines what activity warrants a notification.

Messenger notifications

+ **Who can message you.** Tap to view the following options:

    + Anyone (the default)

    + Your circles

    + Extended circles

+ **Messenger notifications.** Determines whether new messages appear on the status bar.

+ **Vibrate.** Determines whether the mobile device vibrates when new messages appear.

+ **Ringtone.** Enables you to choose a custom ringtone for a Google+ message.

Photo settings

+ **Enable Instant Upload.** With this setting enabled, all photos taken on the smartphone are sent directly to Google+.

+ **When to upload photos.** Choose between Wi-Fi or mobile network or Over Wi-Fi only.

+ **Roaming uploads.** Enables you to upload photos using a data connection (when you're overseas). If you activate it, you can incur significant data charges on your cell phone bill, so I'd leave it unselected.

+ **On battery.** Determines whether photos are uploaded when you are using the battery or only when you are connected to a power source.

+ **Upload all photos.** This option sends all photos currently residing on your phone to Google+.

Press the Back button to return to the Google+ app.

ADJUSTING SETTINGS ON THE iOS APP

Tapping the settings icon in the iOS version of the Google+ app opens the following options:

+ **Sign out.** Tap this to sign out of your Google+ account.

+ **Push notifications.** Tap this to choose what type of Google+ activity warrants a push notification.

+ **Choose stream views.** By default Circles, Incoming, and Nearby Streams are selected. You can choose other Circles you have created from this menu.

+ **Who can message you.** By default everyone can message you, but you can also choose Extended circles and Your circles.

Tap Done to return to the Google+ app.

Viewing Your Stream and Creating Posts in the Google+ App

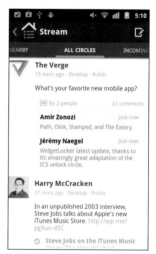

The Stream is where you'll spend most of your time in the Google+ app. To access it, tap Stream. This displays all the recent posts from the All Circles section of the Stream by default (as shown in Figure 13-13).

Swiping up and down enables you to view the recent posts in the Stream, while swiping left and right enables you to view other Streams, including Incoming and Nearby (posts from all Google+ users in the same vicinity as you).

FIGURE 13-13 The Stream in the Google+ app.

CREATING A POST

You can create a post in the Google+ app by following these steps:

1. **Tap Create post icon in the top-right of the screen.**

2. **Tap the + icon to add and remove Circles that you want the post to be shared with (on the iOS version tap the O button).**

3. **Type your message using the keyboard (as shown in Figure 13-14).** It appears in the Type to compose text box (Share your thoughts on the iOS version).

4. **By default your current location is shared.** Tap the location to choose from a list of nearby locations or tap Hide location to remove

the location information. Tap the X button next to the name of your location on the iOS version.

5. **Tap the post (paper plane) icon to share the post (or tap Post on the iOS version).**

You can attach a photo to the post using the camera and photo icons. To take a photo using the phone's built-in camera, follow these steps:

1. **When creating a post, tap the camera icon.**

2. **Line up your shot and tap the shutter button (as shown in Figure 13-15).**

3. **If you're happy with the result, tap OK (Done on some phones, and Use on iOS devices).** Otherwise tap Retake to shoot again.

The image appears as a small icon below the text for the post and is shared on your Stream. If you have Instant Upload switched on, it is automatically sent to your Google+ albums.

You can also share images already in your Google+ photo library by tapping the photo icon, tapping the images you want to include with the post, and tapping Share.

COMMENTING AND SHARING POSTS

When you tap a post, it opens the main window so you can read all the text and view any associated images (as shown in Figure 13-16). All the comments appear below the post and you can add one using the Enter a comment box.

Two icons in the top-right of the screen on an Android phone enable you to +1 or share a post. A Comment box at the bottom of the display enables

FIGURE 13-14 Creating a new post.

FIGURE 13-15 Adding a photo to a post.

you to enter a comment. On an iOS device, only the +1 icon appears at the top, but tapping the arrow icon to the right of the Comment box brings up an option to share the post (as well as Mute this post and Report this post).

Follow these steps to share a post:

1. **Tap Share.**

2. **Tap + next to Your Circles and use the check boxes in the Circles list to select and deselect Circles.**

3. **Enter a message in the Type to compose field.**

4. **Tap the post (paper plane) icon in the top-right of the display.**

FIGURE 13-16 Viewing a post.

If the post was originally shared with a limited group of Circles, a warning message appears (as shown in Figure 13-17). If you are happy to share the post with a wider audience, click OK.

- -

CAN I VIEW CIRCLES OTHER THAN THE DEFAULT THREE? Yes. When you are in the Stream on an Android device, press the Menu button and then tap Select circles. You can add more Streams using the check boxes for the list of all your Circles. On an iOS device, tap the settings (gear) icon on the home page and then tap Choose stream views to display the Circles used in the Stream.

- -

FIGURE 13-17 Sharing a limited post.

Using Messenger in the Google+ App

As its name suggests, the Messenger part of the Google+ app enables you to share messages with other people (as shown in Figure 13-18). It differs from regular instant messaging services or SMS in that you can create conversations with Circles to form group chats. (Google used to call these chats *Huddles* but has recently stopped using the term.)

Follow these steps to start a conversation:

1. **Tap Messenger.**

2. **Tap the new message icon in the top-right of the screen.**

3. **In the Type a name, email, or circle text box, type the name of a person.** If you want to message a Circle, it's easier to tap the + icon to the right and choose Circles from the list.

4. **Type your message into the Type a message box.**

5. **Tap the Send icon.**

A person in the Circle who has not been involved in a message conversation with you previously has to accept your invitation. The person will see an invitation to the conversation (as shown in Figure 13-19) and needs to tap OK before viewing your message.

Once a conversation is underway, everybody involved can type chat replies to each message (as shown in Figure 13-20) and tap the Send icon.

All the different conversations you have taking place appear in the Messenger window, and you can move between one conversation and another by pressing the Back button on the phone.

FIGURE 13-18 Creating a message with a Circle.

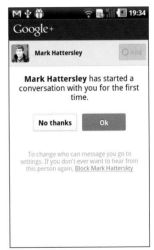

FIGURE 13-19 A message invite.

Pressing the Settings button on the phone during a conversation brings up three options:

+ **Mute.** Tap this option to stop receiving notifications from this conversation (you will still receive the messages). Tap it again to start getting the notifications again.

+ **Hide.** Tap this to hide new messages from the group and no longer receive messages from people involved.

You can add a photo to a message as well. Click the photo icon to the left of the Type a message box and choose either Camera photo or Choose photo. You do this the same way you add a photo to a post, which is discussed earlier in the chapter.

FIGURE 13-20 Replying to messages.

CAN I JOIN A CONVERSATION FROM A DESKTOP? Rather oddly, the answer is no (at the moment). If you're using the Google+ website and a person tries to start a conversation with you from a mobile device (and you don't have the app installed on your phone), then Google sends you a notification prompting you to install the app on your phone.

Viewing and Sharing Photos in the Google+ App

You can view all the photos you have uploaded to Google+ by tapping Photos in the home screen of the Google+ app. This shows all the groups of photos you have in Google+ in a series of square tiles (as shown in Figure 13-21) that rotate between the photos contained within.

The groups are as follows:

FIGURE 13-21 Groups of photos in the Google+ app.

+ From your circles
+ Photos of you
+ From your phone
+ Photos from posts
+ Profile photos

Following these groups are the tiles of all the individual albums you have created for your account.

Tapping on one of the tiles opens the photos contained within (as shown in Figure 13-22). Any photos with comments attached include a small speech bubble icon.

Swiping up and down the screen reveals further photos contained in the album, and tapping on a photo displays it in full screen mode.

You can also swipe left and right on photos to view the next and previous photos contained in the photo library.

Any comments attached to a photo are displayed beneath the image. Tap the photo once to display the comments and to reveal an Enter a comment text box (as shown in Figure 13-23). Tap the photo again to remove the comments and display the image full screen. You can add your own comments using the keyboard and post them using the Send icon. Use the Back button on your smartphone to head back to the albums.

Any photos you have snapped on your mobile phone appear in the From your phone album in Photos on both iOS and Android devices. From here, you can share them with your Circles on Google+.

Follow these steps to share a photo or photos:

1. **Tap Photos.**
2. **Tap the From your phone tile.**

FIGURE 13-22 Viewing a photo album in the Google+ app.

FIGURE 13-23 Viewing comments in the Google+ app.

3. **Tap the circular-arrowed share icon at the bottom of the screen on Android devices.** This step isn't required on iOS devices, which are set to share by default.

4. **Tap to highlight the images that you want to share, as shown in Figure 13-24.** On an iOS device, tap the check boxes below the images.

5. **Tap Share.**

6. **On the Create a post screen, choose which Circles you want to share the image with, and type a message and location information.**

7. **Tap the paper plane–shaped post icon (or tap Post on the iOS devices).**

FIGURE 13-24 Sharing photos from your phone.

Note that this isn't the same as Instant Upload (which automatically syncs photos in From your phone with the From your phone album on the Google+ website). Even if Instant Upload is disabled, the From your phone area of the Google+ app still contains all the photos.

WILL INSTANT UPLOAD WORK ON THE GOOGLE+ iOS APP? If you're using the Google+ app on an iPhone or iPod touch, photos you take are not uploaded to Google+ automatically. Instead, you have to use the Share function before photos are accessible to you on the Google+ website.

Checking Your Profile in the Google+ App

You can also view the information about yourself that is being shared on Google+ by tapping Profile in the Google+ app. This brings up your profile page, as shown in Figure 13-25.

Three tabs enable you to view different parts of your profile:

+ **Posts.** This tab enables you to view recent posts.

+ **About.** This tab takes you to information on your About page.

+ **Photos.** This tab takes you to the Photos page.

The profile page on the Google+ app is pretty limited at the moment. You can't change your About information, and Photos just links to the Photos area as if you'd clicked from the main menu.

Having said that, one thing you can do in the profile page that's pretty handy is delete some of your posts (which is useful if you're out and about and realize a post is getting out of hand). Follow these steps to delete a post:

FIGURE 13-25 Viewing your About details on the profile in the Google+ app.

1. Tap Profile.

2. Tap Posts.

3. Tap the unwanted post.

4. Press the Menu button.

5. Tap Delete.

6. Tap OK.

This deletes the post from the Stream.

Managing Your Circles in the Google+ App

You can also manage your Circles using the Google+ app. You can add and remove people, create new Circles, and delete Circles from within the app (although I find it a lot easier to do serious Circle management in the desktop environment).

Tap Circles to view the Circles screen (as shown in Figure 13-26). Tapping any of the listed Circles displays the people contained in that Circle and tapping a person takes you to his or her profile page (where you can view that person's Posts, About, and Photos pages).

You can also tap the People tab to switch between navigating people by Circles and by a list of individuals.

CAN I BLOCK PEOPLE USING THE GOOGLE+ APP? Yes. If you drill down to a person's About page and press the Menu button, you'll see options for Block and Report abuse.

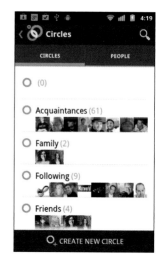

FIGURE 13-26 The Circles screen in the Google+ app.

CREATING A NEW CIRCLE

Follow these steps to create new Circles in the Google+ app:

1. **Tap Circles.**

2. **Tap Create New Circle.** On an iOS device, tap the Circles tab and then tap the +O icon in the top-right of the screen.

3. **Tap Circle name (just Name on an iOS device) and type a name for the Circle (as shown in Figure 13-27).**

4. **Tap OK.**

The new Circle appears in the list (it's in alphabetical order), and is empty, so you need to add people to it.

FIGURE 13-27 Creating a new Circle in the Google+ app.

ADDING PEOPLE TO A CIRCLE

To add people to a Circle in the Google+ app for Android, follow these steps:

1. **Tap a Circle to open it.**

2. **Tap Add People.**

3. **All the people in your Circles appear in a list.** Select the check boxes (as shown in Figure 13-28) next to the people you want in that Circle.

4. **You can search for people in your Circles by tapping the Search icon and entering their names.** You can extend this search to public profiles by tapping Search public profiles. Press the Back button to go back to the Circles.

5. **Tap OK.**

In the Google+ app for iOS devices, you can add people to Circles by tapping on a person's profile and then tapping Add to circles. This also works on Android devices.

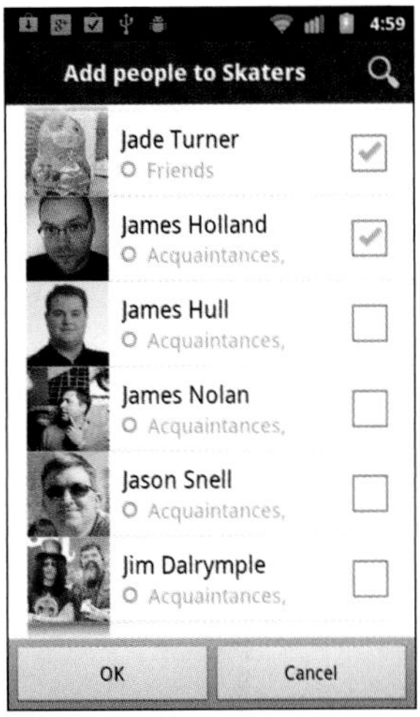

FIGURE 13-28 Adding people to a Circle.

REMOVING PEOPLE FROM A CIRCLE

Follow these steps to remove a person from a Circle in the Google+ app on a Google Android phone:

1. **Tap Circles on the home page.**

2. **Tap a Circle to see the people inside.**

3. **Press the Menu button and tap Remove people (as shown in Figure 13-29).**

4. **Use the check boxes to select people you want to remove.**

5. **Tap OK, and tap OK again.**

On an iOS device, you remove a person from a Circle by opening a profile, clicking the Circles button, removing all check boxes, and tapping Done.

FIGURE 13-29 Removing people from Circles in the Google+ app.

DELETING A CIRCLE

Follow these steps to remove a Circle completely in the Google+ app:

1. **Tap Circles.**

2. **Tap the Circle you want to delete to view the people inside.**

3. **Press the Menu button and tap Delete circle.**

4. **Tap OK (as shown in Figure 13-30).**

The Circle is completely removed. If there are people you only follow in that Circle, they are also removed from your list of contacts. So be careful before deleting whole Circles. There is no undo option for the Google+ app once you have deleted a Circle.

FIGURE 13-30 Deleting a Circle.

Related Questions

+ How do I manage location information? **CHAPTER 6, Adding Location Information**

+ How do I use Circles to create Streams to follow? **CHAPTER 6, Choosing Which Circles to Share Your Posts With**

+ How do I manage my profile? **CHAPTER 2, Completing Your Google+ Profile**

CHAPTER FOURTEEN

WHAT OTHER REALLY COOL GOOGLE+ TRICKS AND TIPS CAN I USE?

In this chapter:

+ Using Google+ with Google Calendar
+ Cool Tricks with Circles
+ Searching within Google+
+ The Best Google+ Extensions
+ Keyboard Shortcuts

A great thing about Google+ is that it's straightforward to use but packs enough functionality to be a powerful service. You can get a complete Google+ experience just by learning how the social network works, which is what the majority of this book covers. But some of you will want to take things a bit further and become power users — people who not only know how to use a service as intended but also have the inside scoop on every little hidden feature and can take the service beyond its original intention.

That's what this chapter is all about: the tricks and tips that turn you from a person who can merely use Google+ to somebody who rocks it.

Using Google+ with Google Calendar

One of the biggest limitations of Google+ (at least for the time being) is that it lacks the functionality to create and manage events. This is a bit odd given that Google Calendar is a hugely powerful and popular web application for doing exactly that.

I imagine Google won't waste too much time before rolling Calendar into Google+, but if you really can't wait for Google+ to get Calendar functionality, it is fairly easy to create events in Calendar and share them with your Circles.

First you need to create a public calendar that other people are able to view. Follow these steps:

1. **Hover your mouse over the Google menu in the Google+ bar, click More, and then choose Calendar.**

2. **Click the gear icon in the top-right of the window and choose Settings.**

3. **Click Calendars and then click Create new calendar.**

4. **Type a relevant name into the Calendar Name box.** You can also give it a description if you want (as shown in Figure 14-1).

5. **Select the Make this calendar public check box and click Create Calendar.**

6. **A warning appears that your public calendar is visible to everyone in the world.** Click Yes.

This creates a new calendar that appears in the Google Calendar sidebar (below My calendars).

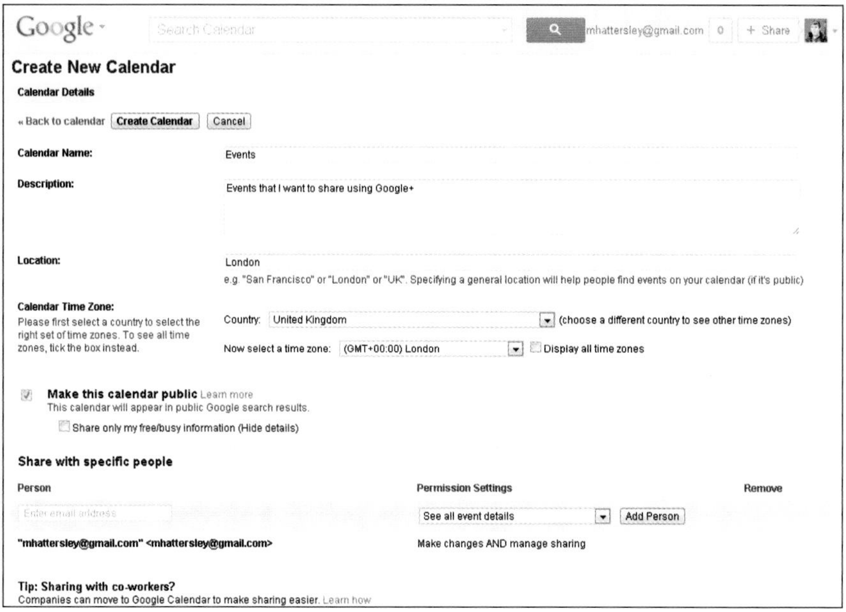

FIGURE 14-1 Creating a calendar in Google+.

Once you have created the calendar, you need to create an event to share on Google+.

You need to stay in Google Calendar to create events before sharing them on Google+. Follow these steps to create an event:

1. **Click the red Create button in the left-hand column.**

2. **Enter the details for the event (as shown in Figure 14-2).**

3. **Click the Calendar drop-down list and choose the calendar that you have created especially for sharing.** Now click Save.

4. **Click on the event in the Calendar and choose Edit event.** This reopens the event details page with a new option at the bottom called Publish event.

5. **Click Publish event.** This opens a window with a long piece of HTML text (as shown in Figure 14-3). Select all the text, right-click, and choose Copy.

6. **Open Google+ and click in the Share what's new box to create a new post.** Type some details about the event.

7. **Click the link icon in the post and paste the link into the text box.** Click Add and a Google Calendar description appears in the post (as shown in Figure 14-4).

FIGURE 14-2 Creating a new event.

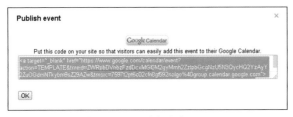

FIGURE 14-3 Obtaining a public link to an event.

The people you share the event with can click the link, which opens their version of Google Calendar, containing the event details (the same details you created in Step 2). When they click Save, the event is added to their version of Google Calendar.

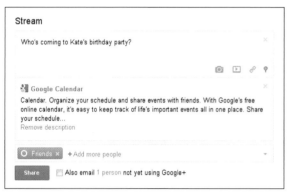

FIGURE 14-4 Sharing an event in Google+.

Cool Tricks with Circles

In my mind, Circles is the single coolest feature of Google+. It makes so much more sense than having the standard list of friends in Facebook. And there's a lot you can do with Circles in Google+ beyond just organizing people into regular groups.

ORGANIZING YOUR LIST OF CIRCLES

You can drag and drop Circles in the Circles window to rearrange them (as shown in Figure 14-5). This also determines the order that they appear in the left-hand column (the left-to-right order in the Circles window corresponds to the vertical list of the left-hand column). If you have lots of Circles, it's easier to organize the most frequently used ones at the top (as shown in Figure 14-6). This makes them easier to click and view.

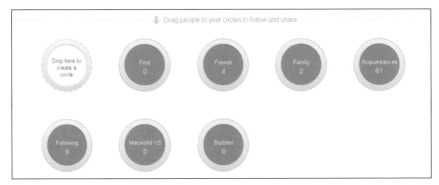

FIGURE 14-5 Rearranging Circles.

CREATING A SAVED CIRCLE

A really neat trick is to create a custom Circle that you can use to save posts that you find interesting. You use it to keep a record of cool posts (and the web pages they link to) so you can browse through them at a later date.

Follow these steps to create a Saved Circle:

1. **Click Circles.**

2. **Hover the mouse over Drop here to create a circle and click Create circle.**

3. **Give the Circle the name Saved.**

4. **Click Add a new person (as shown in Figure 14-7) and enter your name in the Find by name or email box.** Do not add anybody else to the Circle.

5. **Click Create circle with 1 person.**

FIGURE 14-6 The list of Circles in the left-hand column.

Now when you want to keep a record of a post, click Share and remove any Circles from the list. Click Add more people and enter the Saved Circle to the list (you can add other Circles if you also want to share the post). Click Share.

Now when you want to view the saved posts, you choose Saved from the left-hand column. The Stream will contain all the posts that you've shared with yourself, and nobody else will be able to view them.

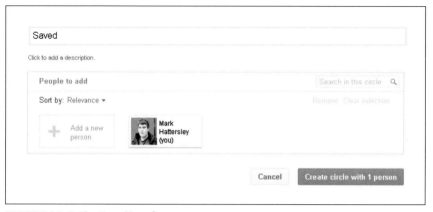

FIGURE 14-7 The Saved list of posts.

If you want to remove posts from the Saved list, click the arrow in the top-right of the post and choose Delete this post.

CIRCLE SCROLLING

If you have a Circle with more than 30 people in it, use this trick to spin the faces around on the Circle page. Hover your mouse over the Circle so the profile pictures appear on the outside, and use your mouse scroll wheel to spin up and down. (Google+ doesn't remember the position of the people, unfortunately.)

Searching within Google+

Search is pretty central to a lot of what Google does, so it's no surprise to learn that there are a couple of neat tricks that combine Google's search technology with Google+.

You can search the Google+ website in Google Search by entering your search term and then **site:plus.google.com.** This limits the search to just the Google+ website. The site: term can also be used to search any single website.

If you want to frequently search in Google+, you can set up Google Chrome (but no other web browser) with custom search terms. Two good ones to use are **posts** and **profiles,** which search through Google+ posts and profiles accordingly. Follow these steps to set up these custom Google+ searches in Google Chrome:

1. **In Google Chrome, click the wrench icon and choose Options.**
2. **Click Basics and Manage search engines.**
3. **In the Add a new search engine text box, type** Google+ posts.
4. **In the Keyword text box, type** posts.
5. **In the URL With %s in place of query text box, type** {google:baseURL}search?q=site:plus.google.com inurl:posts/* %s.
6. **If you've entered the terms correctly, the new search term is added to the list of Other search engines.**
7. **You need to repeat the process for the profiles search.** In the Add a new search engine text box, type **Google+ profiles.**
8. **In the Keyword text box, type** profiles.
9. **In the URL with %s in place of query text box, type** {google:baseURL} search?q=%s&tbs=prfl:e. The screen should look like Figure 14-8.

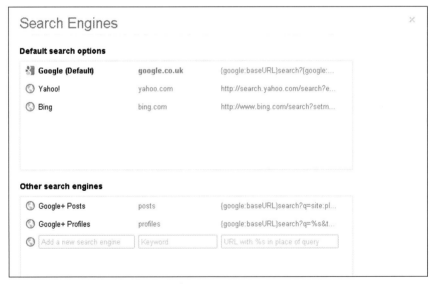

FIGURE 14-8 Adding custom search engines.

Now when you want to search Google posts, type the term **posts** followed by the search term in the Google Chrome search bar. A blue search icon appears to signify that you are performing a custom search. You use the second search term (for profiles) in the same way: by starting any search with the word **profiles.**

The Best Google+ Extensions

A great way to expand your Google+ experience is to install Google Chrome extensions. These are small programs that add custom functionality to the Google Chrome web browser, which you can install via the Chrome Web Store (https://chrome.google.com/webstore).

In the Chrome Web Store, click Extensions in the sidebar to display a list of extensions you can install.

Select an extension to view its details (as shown in Figure 14-9), click Add to Chrome, and then click Install to add it to your browser. The extension quickly and quietly installs (there is no need to refresh or restart your browser).

FIGURE 14-9 Installing an extension in Chrome.

You can browse for extensions or use the built-in search engine to find useful ones. Here are some great Google+ extensions to search for:

- **Google +1 Button.** This extension adds a +1 button to the Chrome Toolbar (to the left of the settings icon), enabling you to easily +1 any page you want.

- **Google+ Notifications.** This extension enables you to view notifications of Google+ activity in the Chrome browser no matter which website you are looking at.

- **G+ Extended.** This extension adds some extra shortcuts to Google+.

- **Replies and more for Google+.** This extension adds extra buttons that enable you to reply to individual people (such as the author of a post).

- **+Photo Zoom.** This extension enables you to zoom in on photos and profile images inside the Google+ Stream by hovering the mouse over the image (as shown in Figure 14-10).

FIGURE 14-10 Extensions add new functionality to Google+, like this photo zoom.

+ **Helper for Google+.** This extension adds a bunch of extra features, including the ability to tweet posts direct to Twitter, as well as bookmark Google+ posts and translate posts with Google Translate.

+ **Extended Share For Google Plus.** Sharing posts on Google+ is all well and good, but this extension enables you to also share them on Facebook, LinkedIn, Twitter, and other social networks.

+ **Google Translate for Google+.** This extension uses Google Translate technology to convert languages in posts so you can follow people posting in languages you don't understand.

+ **Layouts for Google Plus.** If you want to personalize Google+, this extension enables you to change the background to any image you want.

Hundreds of other extensions are available for Google+, with new ones being developed and released all the time. You can search for them on the Chrome Web Store.

WHY DOES SEARCHING FOR GOOGLE+ JUST RETURN RESULTS FOR GOOGLE? Because the plus sign is a boolean search term (it means AND in most search engines, including Google), and because all words in searches are by default designated as AND searches. So the + is disregarded from the search term. If you type **Google+ iPhone** into Google Search, it recognizes the search term as Google AND iPhone, and returns results from every page with Google mentioned in it. If you put Google+ in quote marks (**"Google+"**), the plus sign is included and you get results from the Google+ website.

Keyboard Shortcuts

Learning to use keyboard shortcuts can make your Google+ experience a lot better. You can use keyboard shortcuts to move quickly around posts and write comments without having to reach for the mouse. Shortcuts make your Google+ experience faster and more fun.

Here are some keyboard shortcuts you should become familiar with:

+ **J and K.** Use J and K keys to move up and down through posts.

+ **Tab and Enter.** Press Enter to open a post and start writing a comment. Press Tab and Enter (or Return on a Mac) again to click the Post comment button.

+ **Arrow keys.** You can also use the arrow keys to navigate up and down the Google+ notifications. Pressing left and right also drills in and out of notification details. It is also possible to use J, K, and Enter to navigate notifications (although I find using the arrow keys easier).

+ **Spacebar and Shift+spacebar.** You can scroll up and down the Stream (as with most web browsers) by pressing the spacebar to go down and Shift+spacebar to move up.

+ **@ and +.** You can quickly mention a person in a post by typing **@** or **+** and then a name. Choose the right person from the pop-up menu (as shown in Figure 14-11). The person appears in your post as a clickable link to his profile.

Getting to know these shortcuts enables you to use Google+ a bit faster and have more fun.

FIGURE 14-11 Quickly tag people to a post with the @ symbol.

GET MORE KEYBOARD SHORTCUTS

You can get more keyboard shortcuts by installing the G+ Extended extension from the Chrome Web Store (https://chrome.google.com/webstore). When it is installed, the following additional keyboard shortcuts are available:

+ **+.** Press + to +1 a post.

+ **-.** Press - to remove a +1 from a post.

+ **P.** Press P to toggle the +1 on a post.

+ **S.** Press S to share a post.

+ **E.** Press E to expand a post.

These shortcuts work when you have a post in focus. You can get a post in focus by clicking it or pressing J, K, and Enter.

Related Questions

+ How do I manage my Circles? **CHAPTER 5, Editing and Sharing Circle Information**

+ How do I view posts? **CHAPTER 3, Looking at Your Stream**

+ How do I use +1? **CHAPTER 10, Recommending Articles and Posts with +1**

CHAPTER FIFTEEN

HOW DO I MANAGE MY PRIVACY AND PERSONAL INFORMATION?

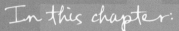

In this chapter:

+ Discovering Just How Much Google Knows About You

+ Looking at the Privacy Center

+ Choosing What Information You Want to Make Public

+ Looking at the Google Dashboard

+ Accessing a Deceased Person's Gmail Account

+ Deleting Your Google Account

When you share so much of your personal information with services like Google+, Facebook, and Twitter, one rather big question arises: How private is it?

Obviously, the information you're posting publicly isn't private in any sense. But what about your email, cell phone number, home address, and work information? And that's before you consider the information on your private life.

Once you start to think about it, quite a few questions spring to mind: Just how much information are you sharing with companies? What are they doing with it? Who are they, in turn, sharing it with? How secure is your personal information from unintentional sharing or hacking? Exactly what have you permitted these companies to do with it? And why do they want it?

These are all valid questions. Even more so when you stop to think about just how closely you read the Terms of Service when you signed up for Google. You did read it, right? Chances are you didn't. Very few people truly read these things before clicking Accept.

Discovering Just How Much Google Knows About You

When you start to investigate Google (or Facebook and other services), you suddenly realize that the company knows an awful lot about you. And that Google is using this information primarily to build an accurate profile of who you are and what you like. This way it can effectively target its advertising; that is, it sends you ads for products and services that you're interested in.

Obviously, some people are more relaxed about this than others. At the Google Zeitgeist forum in 2010, Google Executive Chairman Eric Schmidt told the audience that "Society as a group has not decided what is appropriate and what is not appropriate in the privacy sphere, and each society and group will differ." I'd take it even further and say that most *individuals* will differ.

Only the year previously, in 2009, Schmidt also said, "If you have something that you don't want anyone to know, maybe you shouldn't be doing it in the first place." In which case, you might want to ask him if he has curtains in his home.

CAN I READ MY TERMS OF SERVICE AGAIN? Yes, of course. Just visit www.google.com/policies/terms to see plenty of information from Google regarding privacy.

Google does take privacy very seriously, however, and lists five privacy principles that describe how it approaches user information:

1. **Use information to provide our users with valuable products and services.**

2. **Develop products that reflect strong privacy standards and practices.**

3. **Make the collection of personal information transparent.**

4. **Give users meaningful choices to protect their privacy.**

5. **Be a responsible steward of the information we hold.**

These are all noble statements, although there's no doubt that Google owns a lot of information about you. Go to www.google.com/about/company/privacy_principles.html for more information.

As for me, I'm quite happy for Google to try to work out who I am, what I do, and what I like if it means I get to watch ads for the latest blockbuster video games (which I like) and not for independent French movies (which I'm by-and-large indifferent to). But some people might feel differently about Google having all that information on them, and rightly so. And even if you're not that concerned about all your personal details being online, it's always interesting to figure out what Google knows about you and where the information came from. Google has a single integrated privacy policy for most of its products; you can read it online at www.google.com/policies/privacy.

IS GOOGLE TRACKING ME WHEN I'M NOT LOGGED IN? Yes, through the use of cookies and your IP address, Google (and other services and websites) can track you even when you're not logged in. When you are logged in, Google connects your activity to your profile. Later in this chapter you learn about cookies and private browsing.

As you'd expect, Google tracks information on people from all its products: Google+, Gmail, Calendar, and so on. Here are some of the things you might not expect that Google is monitoring:

+ **Google Search.** Everything you type into it as well as a lot of information on the results.

+ **Google Personalized Search.** A log of every website you visit as a result of a search.

+ **Google account.** Everything you enter into an account when you sign up.

+ **Toolbar.** All websites you visit as well as returning data on a site's performance.

+ **Google Translate.** All the text you enter.

+ **Google Finance.** Your stock portfolio.

+ **Google Checkout.** Your name, credit card number, and debit card number.

+ **YouTube.** All the videos you have uploaded, watched, and commented on.

+ **Gmail.** All your email messages, as well as all the activity on those emails (links that are clicked, for example).

+ **Google Docs.** Email address, clicks, collaborators, and all text and images.

+ **Clicks.** Every navigational click on all Google services.

+ **Server requests.** Tracks your IP address, date, language, search query, operating system, and browser every time you access any Google.com site.

Danny Dover from website SEOmoz has created a pretty impressive list of all the things that Google is tracking at www.seomoz.org/blog/the-evil-side-of-google-exploring-googles-user-data-collection#list. It makes for some interesting (and exhaustive) reading. This chapter explains how you can manage this impressive list of information that Google is gathering about you.

THIS IS PRETTY COMPLEX STUFF. IS IT EXPLAINED ANYWHERE?
Google has created a couple of sites to explain its privacy policy in clearer detail: Google Good to Know (www.google.com/goodtoknow) and Google Family Safety Center (www.google.com/familysafety).

WHO DOES GOOGLE THINK YOU ARE?

So what does Google think of you? It won't come as much of a surprise that Google has a pretty accurate map of who you are.

One of the really good things about Google, however, is that it's pretty open about enabling you to access the information it has on you. And you can edit or delete this information if you think it's incorrect.

A good place to discover what Google thinks of you is the Google Ads Preferences Manager, which can be found at www.google.com/ads/preferences. The Ads Preferences Manager (as shown in Figure 15-1) gives a good overview of what Google thinks are your interests. If you have only just started using a new Internet browser and Google has no information, you see information regarding Google ads in general and a link enabling you to remove or edit these.

As you can see in the figure, here's some of what Google says about me:

+ **Arts & Entertainment** - Music and Audio - Urban & Hip Hop - Rap & Hip Hop

+ **Business & Industrial** - Industrial Materials & Equipment

+ **Computers & Electronics** - Software - Operating Systems - Mac OS

+ **Games** - Computers & Video Games

+ **Internet & Telecom** - Search Engines

+ **News** - Technology News

+ **Online Communities** - Social Networks

And this is my demographic:

+ **Age:** 35-44

+ **Gender:** Male

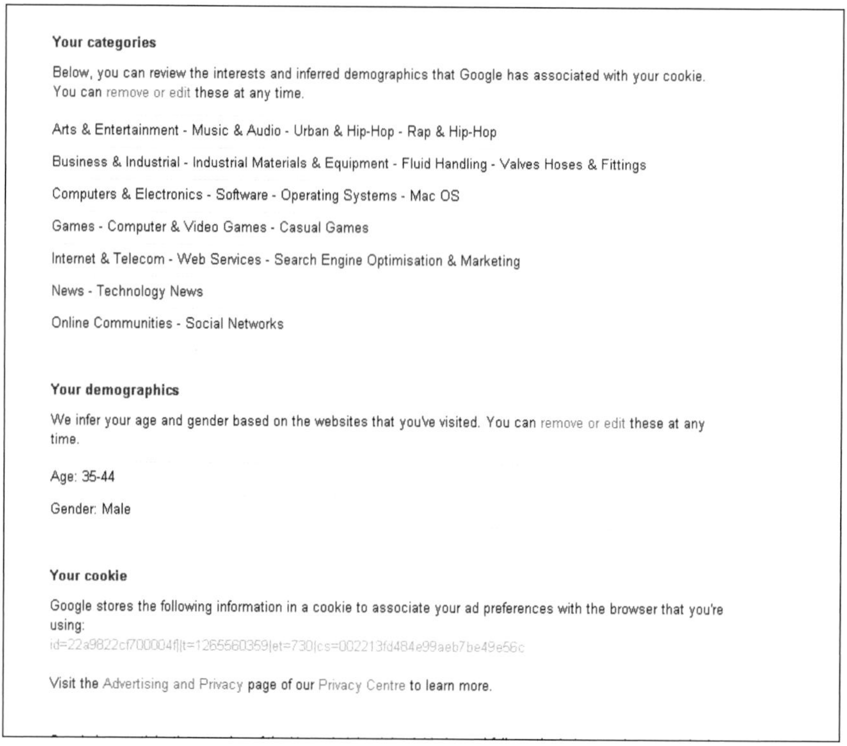

Your categories

Below, you can review the interests and inferred demographics that Google has associated with your cookie. You can remove or edit these at any time.

Arts & Entertainment - Music & Audio - Urban & Hip-Hop - Rap & Hip-Hop

Business & Industrial - Industrial Materials & Equipment - Fluid Handling - Valves Hoses & Fittings

Computers & Electronics - Software - Operating Systems - Mac OS

Games - Computer & Video Games - Casual Games

Internet & Telecom - Web Services - Search Engine Optimisation & Marketing

News - Technology News

Online Communities - Social Networks

Your demographics

We infer your age and gender based on the websites that you've visited. You can remove or edit these at any time.

Age: 35-44

Gender: Male

Your cookie

Google stores the following information in a cookie to associate your ad preferences with the browser that you're using:

id=22a9822cf700004f|t=1265560359|et=730|cs=002213fd484e99aeb7be49e56c

Visit the Advertising and Privacy page of our Privacy Centre to learn more.

FIGURE 15-1 The Ads Preferences Manager.

I'd say Google has pretty much nailed me, but if you think something is wrong with your Google Ads Preferences, you can always change them.

EDITING YOUR AD PREFERENCES

If you think some of this information is wrong, it's possible to remove and add categories and remove your demographic. Do the following:

1. **Open Ads Preferences (www.google.com/ads/preferences) in your browser.**

2. **Click remove or edit under Your categories or Your demographics.**

3. **The list of categories appears (as shown in Figure 15-2).** Click Remove next to any you don't want.

4. **Demographics are listed at the bottom.** Click Remove if you want to delete these.

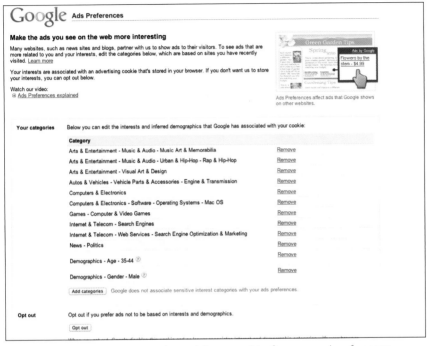

FIGURE 15-2 Removing categories and demographics from your ad preferences.

If you want, you can also add new categories and demographics:

1. **Open Ads Preferences and click remove or edit.**

2. **Click Add categories.**

3. **The categories are in nested lists.** Click the + sign next to a category to see subcategories (as shown in Figure 15-3).

4. **Click Add next to a category you want.**

5. **Click Submit.**

It should be noted that this information is based on a cookie (a small file) associated with your web browser, not your Google account. So if you try it from a fresh browser or have cookies turned off, Google won't have this information.

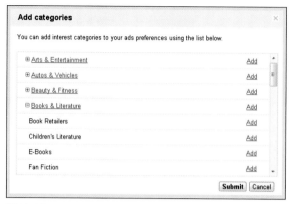

FIGURE 15-3 Adding categories and demographics to your ad preferences.

OPTING OUT OF AD PREFERENCES

If you're not happy with Google forming an ad-based profile of you and would rather Google didn't serve ads based on your interests and demographics, you can opt out of the system:

1. **Open Ads Preferences (www.google.com/ads/preferences) in your browser.**

2. **Click Opt out in the left-hand column and then click Opt out.** This only removes you from receiving customized Google ads on the web. You still receive customized advertising within Google services like Gmail, and you still see ads on the web, which may be customized by services other than Google.

3. **Click Ads on Search and Gmail (as shown in Figure 15-4).**

4. **Click Opt out in the left-hand column and click Opt out.**

You can opt in at any time by returning to Google Ads Preferences and clicking Opt in.

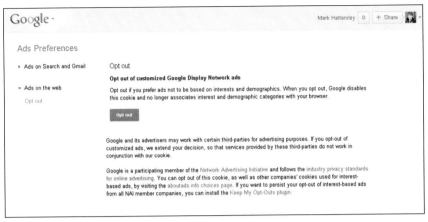

FIGURE 15-4 Opting out of Google Ads Preferences.

DISABLING COOKIES AND OTHER OPTIONS

If you want to opt out of allowing Google to track your information via a cookie in your browser, you might want to consider taking things a step further and ensuring that you aren't allowing other sites to take advantage of cookies to track your movements.

There are two ways to do this. The first is to install a plug-in called *Keep My Opt-Outs* in the Google Chrome browser (this does not work with other browsers). Keep My Opt-Outs ensures that all members of the Network Advertising Initiative (www.networkadvertising.org) do not use cookies to personalize ads. The second method is to disable cookies in your browser. Follow these steps to install Keep My Opt-Outs:

1. **Open the Chrome Web Store (https://chrome.google.com/webstore).**

2. **Search for Keep My Opt-Outs.**

3. **Click Add To Chrome.** (If you are using a browser other than Chrome, you see an Available on Chrome button.)

This opts you out of personalized advertising and data tracking by all supported companies.

Of course, not all companies are members of the Network Advertising Initiative, so you might want to take things a step further by disabling the use of cookies in your web browser. Here's how to do this in Google Chrome:

1. **Click the wrench-shaped Customize and Control Google Chrome icon in the top-right of the browser, and choose Options.**

2. **Click Under the Hood (Under The Bonnet in some locations) in the left-hand column.**

3. **Click Content Settings.** You see these options (as shown in Figure 15-5):

   + **Allow local data to be set (recommended).** This enables websites to store information on you.

   + **Allow local data to be set for the current session only.** When you close the web browser, all local data is cleared.

   + **Block sites from setting any data.**

   + **Block third-party cookies from being set.**

   + **Clear cookies and other site and plug-in data when I close my browser.**

4. **If you want to stop cookies completely, choose Block sites from setting any data and select the two check boxes.**

5. **Close and restart the Chrome web browser.**

Personally, I find turning off all cookies a bit extreme. They are used for a variety of purposes (not just tracking users for advertising), such as remembering your login details, personalizing websites, and serving up individualized content. Cookies can make the web experience a lot better.

If you want to manage cookies more closely, you can click Manage exceptions to turn on cookie activity for certain sites. Click All cookies and site data to see what cookies are available.

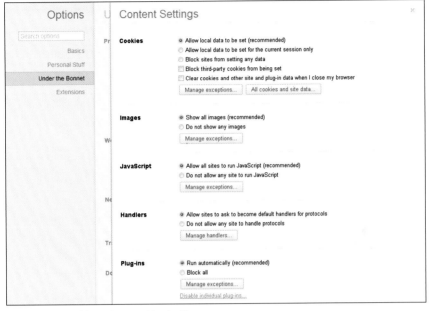

FIGURE 15-5 Managing cookies in Chrome.

Looking at the Privacy Center

So far, you've looked at general information that Google uses to keep track of you. But it is possible to manage and check all your information in the Google Privacy Center, which provides a set of privacy tools.

The Privacy Center, which you can find at www.google.com/privacy/tools.html, has tools that are used to manage your information on Google. The following tools are available:

+ **Google Dashboard.** See and check all the information that Google knows about you.

+ **Ads Preferences Manager.** View and edit the information Google uses to manage ads (as outlined earlier in the chapter).

+ **Data Liberation Front.** Move your data in and out of Google. Chapter 12 has information on how to liberate your data.

+ **Keep My Opt-Outs.** This Chrome extension provides persistent opting out of ads (also outlined earlier in the chapter).

+ **Encrypted search.** Enables you to encrypt the traffic between you and Google for more secure searching.

+ **Incognito mode in Google Chrome.** Information on how to browse without web history or downloads being recorded. Press Shift+Control+N to open a new browser window incognito mode.

+ **Street View Blurring and Takedowns.** Request blurring of images in Street View that feature you, your family, your car, or home as well as inappropriate content.

+ **Unlisted and Private Videos on YouTube.** Information on keeping videos private on YouTube.

+ **Web History Controls.** Enables you to view, delete, and control entries on web history. You can also opt out of having your web history recorded completely.

+ **Off the Record Gmail Chats.** Information on how to have chats in Gmail without them being recorded.

+ **Google Analytics Opt-out.** Instructions on how to install an opt-out so your visits are no longer recorded on Google Analytics (the service that Google provides to websites so they can track visitors).

+ **Search Personalization Opt-out.** Disables Google from personalizing search results based on what you are likely to be looking for.

+ **Control Your Location in Google Latitude.** Adjust privacy settings so you share less information about your location.

Despite collecting a phenomenal amount of information on people, Google appears to be fairly transparent about having that information. It provides you with detailed access to all the data it holds on you and tools to opt out of data collection, and it makes it easy for you to change and delete certain aspects of its data (as well as your whole account).

Choosing What Information You Want to Make Public

Google+ is geared toward helping you determine what information you want to make public. Google+'s approach to sharing information using Circles is, in itself, a means to ensuring that the information you share is kept to a limited audience. Be sure to keep an eye on your Circles and make sure you are sharing the right information with the right group of people.

If you're sharing a private piece of information with a limited Circle, take time to lock the post (as shown in Figure 15-6). This prevents people in your Circles from resharing the post with other people. Chapter 5 has more information on setting up Circles.

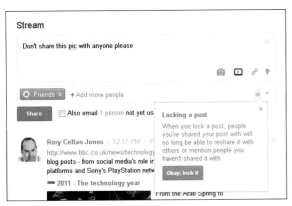

FIGURE 15-6 Locking a post.

HOW CAREFUL SHOULD I BE ABOUT SHARING PRIVATE INFORMATION? Google+ is great at offering you control over who you share information with, but I still subscribe to the point of view that if you really don't want people to know something, don't write about it online.

USING THE GOOGLE+ PROFILE AND PRIVACY SETTINGS

Beyond using Circles to manage what content you share online, Google+ also has a group of settings and features that you can use to check and manage your privacy.

Click the account icon on the Google+ bar and choose Privacy to open the privacy settings (as shown in Figure 15-7). You can use the settings here to check on your Google profile and how it appears when you are searched for online. You can also access your Circles and Profile settings, where you can edit what information is available to other people.

Chapter 12 has more information on using profile and privacy settings.

FIGURE 15-7 Profile and privacy settings.

EDITING YOUR PROFILE VISIBILITY

Your Google+ profile (accessed by clicking the account icon) represents the information on you that both you and other people can see. Chapter 2 has more information on setting up your Google+ profile, but you might have overlooked that you can control who in your Circles can view what types of information about you.

You can granularly control it by editing your profile. Follow these steps to determine what information is visible to whom in your profile:

1. **Click your account icon in the Google+ bar and choose Profile.**

2. **Click Edit Profile.**

3. **Click Introduction to reveal the edit mode for that area (as shown in Figure 15-8).**

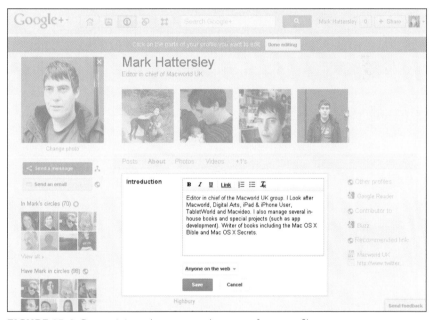

FIGURE 15-8 Determining who can see elements of your profile.

4. **Click the Who can see this? drop-down list and choose from the following options:**

   + Anyone on the web

   + Extended circles

   + Your circles

   + Only you

   + Custom

5. **Click Save.**

6. **Click Done editing.**

You can repeat this process for all the different elements on the About page, determining exactly who can see what parts of your profile.

You can also edit privacy settings for other elements on the profile. When you click Edit Profile on the Photos page of your profile (as shown in Figure 15-9), the following settings are available:

+ **Show this tab on your profile.** This option (selected by default) enables people to see your photos when viewing your profile.

+ **Allow viewers to download my photos.** This option (selected by default) enables people to copy the image files to their computer.

+ **Find my face in photos and prompt people I know to tag me.** With this default option on, people are notified when Google thinks you appear in a photo. The person uploading the photo is prompted to confirm your name and tag you in the photo. This uses Google's face-recognition technology.

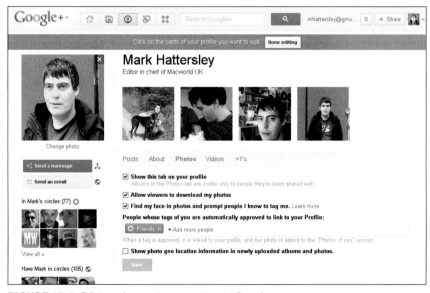

FIGURE 15-9 Editing photo privacy settings in Google+.

+ **People whose tags of you are automatically approved to link to your profile.** This option enables you to determine which people can tag you in a photo. The default setting is Friends.

+ **Show photo geo location information in newly uploaded albums and photos.** This option (unselected by default) shows any photo geo location, which is usually added when you use a smartphone camera or a camera with location-service technology, such as GPS. So people can see not just your pictures but also a map of where they were taken.

What settings you enable or disable is very much a personal choice. I show my photos on my profile and allow viewers to download my photos, but I'm wary of allowing tagging. I am happy for my photos to show geo location information, however.

Both the Videos and +1's pages of the profile also contain the Show this tab on your profile check box, enabling you to hide videos and +1's alongside photos from public viewing. However, you cannot assign your photos, videos, and +1's to Circles — it's an all or nothing situation.

DETERMINING WHO CAN SEND YOU MESSAGES AND EMAILS

You can also use the edit mode on the profile page to determine who can send you messages. By default, anybody in your Extended Circles can send a message to you (that's anybody who is one degree away from you; that is, in a Circle of a person who is in your Circles) and anybody can send you an email.

Follow these steps to change this setting:

1. **Click Profile and then click Edit Profile.**

2. **Click Send a message to view the settings (as shown in Figure 15-10).**

3. **Select the Who can send you a message? check box to enable people to message you using the link on your profile.**

4. **Click the Who can see this? drop-down list and choose from the following:**

   + Anyone on the web

   + Extended circles

> ✛ Your circles
> ✛ Only you
> ✛ Custom

5. Click Save.

You can repeat this process for the Send an email settings.

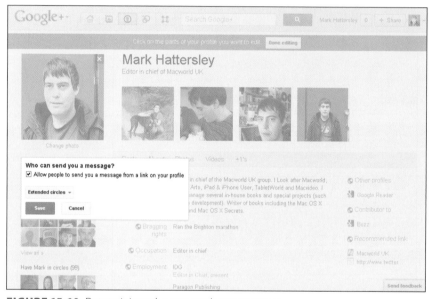

FIGURE 15-10 Determining who can send you messages.

DETERMINING WHO CAN SEE YOUR CIRCLES

In the left-hand column of your profile are two areas that relate to your Circles: In *YourName's* circles and Have *YourName* in circles. These display photos of eight people from your Circles plus links to view everyone in your Circles.

You can use the Edit Profile feature to control the visibility of this information:

1. Click Profile and then click Edit Profile.

2. Click the Circles box in the left-hand column. This reveals the following options (as shown in Figure 15-11):

+ **Show people in.** Deselect this check box to hide the people in your Circles completely.

+ **All circles.** Use this drop-down list to choose people from specific Circles to appear in your profile.

+ **Who can see this?** Two options are available: Anyone on the web and Your circles.

+ **Show people who have added you to circles.**

3. **Click Save and then click Done editing.**

You can use the View profile as text box to check how your profile appears to other people. Choose a person from your Circles or click on Anyone on the web.

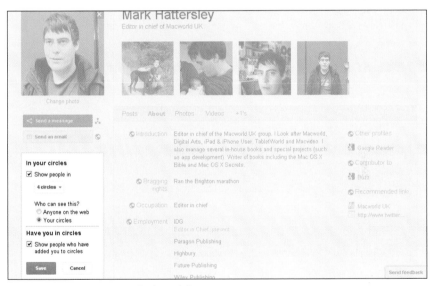

FIGURE 15-11 Managing Circle visibility.

CAN PEOPLE SEE WHICH CIRCLE THEY ARE IN? Your Circles are always private. Although people can see whether they are in your Circles (and vice versa), there is no information about which Circle they are in.

Looking at the Google Dashboard

You can use the Google Dashboard (www.google.com/dashboard) to access a wide range of personal information about you that Google is holding (as shown in Figure 15-12). You can also use it for a range of services. Here are some of the things you can do in the Google Dashboard:

+ **Account.** Manage your account, edit personal information, and change your password.

+ **Me on the Web.** Set up search alerts (email alerts when people post information about you online), manage your online identity, and request that Google removes unwanted content.

+ **Profile.** Edit your profile, manage the sharing of contact info, and view privacy policies.

+ **AdSense.** Manage your AdSense account (if you have one with Google).

+ **Alerts.** Set up alerts for when people search for certain key terms in Google.

+ **Analytics.** Manage your Google Analytics settings (if you have a web-site with Google Analytics).

+ **Android devices.** View a list of which Google Android–based devices you have associated with your account.

+ **Gmail.** Manage Chat history.

+ **Google Sync.** Check which devices are syncing with Google notifica-tions. You may not see this if you have no devices syncing with Google (Android devices such as smartphones do not show up in this part of the window; they are in the Android devices section instead).

+ **Google+.** Click links to edit your profile and Circles.

There are also a lot of other Google services included with direct links to managing account settings and private information. Most of these settings are located within the Google services themselves, but Google Dashboard is a good place to get an overview of all the different options available.

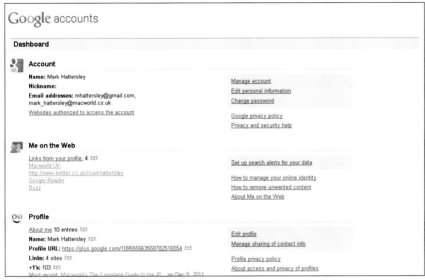

FIGURE 15-12 The Google Dashboard.

Accessing a Deceased Person's Gmail Account

Although it might not be the first thing that springs to your mind, there may come a time (unfortunately) when somebody you know passes away and the question of what to do with his or her online identity arises.

You may also wish to access a deceased person's email for legal and personal reasons. Google has a service set up to handle this, although because of the nature of the request, it is handled individually rather than by an automated service.

You need to supply the following to Google:

+ Your name.

+ Your mailing address.

+ Your email address.

+ A photocopy of a government-issued ID (driver's license, passport, and so on).

+ The Gmail address of the deceased user.

+ The death certificate of the deceased user.

+ The following information from a Gmail message you received from the deceased person's account:

    + The full header from the email message.

    + The entire content of the message.

Google asks that you mail or fax this information to its headquarters:

Google Inc.

Gmail User Support - Decedents' Accounts

c/o Google Custodian of Records

1600 Amphitheatre Parkway

Mountain View, CA 94043

Fax: 650-644-0358

Google personnel review the request and notify you by email how to proceed. The whole process is reputed to be quite slow, taking at least 30 days to even get started.

Deleting Your Google Account

One final and rather extreme approach to privacy with Google is to delete your account completely. Take note that doing this means you are no longer able to use any of the Google products associated with that account.

Follow these steps to delete an account:

1. **Visit https://accounts.google.com/b/1/DeleteAccount.**

2. **Sign in to the Google account.** If you have more than one account, be careful to check the account details carefully in the top-right of the screen.

3. **Select all the check boxes in the screen (as shown in Figure 15-13) next to each service that will be deleted along with your account.**

4. **Type your password into the Current password text box.**

FIGURE 15-13 Deleting your Google account.

5. Select the Yes, I want to delete my account check box.

6. Select the Yes, I acknowledge that I am still responsible for any charges incurred due to any pending financial transactions check box.

7. Click Delete Google Account.

And just like that, it's all gone. You see a message on screen stating that your account has been deleted.

CAN I RECOVER MY ACCOUNT ONCE IT'S BEEN DELETED? Google does offer an account recovery service, which depends on your passing a knowledge test about the account. There are no guarantees, though. More information is available at www.google.com/accounts/recovery/knowledgetest?hl=en. Enter the email and password, and click submitting a recovery request. If you pass the test, you are sent a link by email to reactivate the account.

Related Questions

+ How do I add personal information to my profile? **CHAPTER 2, Completing Your Google+ Profile**

+ How do I block people in Google+? **CHAPTER 5, Blocking People**

+ How do I manage Google+ privacy settings? **CHAPTER 12, Managing Profile and Privacy Settings**

+ How do I get a hold of all the information that Google has on me? **CHAPTER 12, Accessing Data Liberation**

HOW DO I USE GOOGLE+ TO PROMOTE MY BUSINESS?

I f you work with a business, brand, or group (like a sports fan club or band), then you really want to take a look at Google+ Pages. You can use Pages to promote your services and events, offer news, and connect directly with your customers, fans, or followers. Just like your own account, Pages have their own profile and Circles, and you can upload photos and videos on a Page as well as create posts and share other posts.

In many ways, Pages on Google+ is really similar to your own account, and once you've set it up, you'll find using Pages a breeze.

Understanding Google's Approach to Businesses on Google+

At its heart, Google+ is all about people and the relationships between people, and Pages is no exception. Although you create a Page for an organization, it connects your organization with customers (which is one reason businesses are so excited about it). You can connect through posts and comments in the Stream as well as uploaded photos and videos, but what has got businesses really excited is Hangouts. This Google+ feature allows representatives of a brand or organization to have live video conversations with their customers, just as you can join in with live chats with your friends.

As Google says in the Pages introduction video, "Businesses don't make people happy. People do." Google+ Pages is about connecting brands with people. For example, Figure 16-1 displays the Google+ Pepsi Page, which promotes Pepsi products.

There are some key differences between individual profiles and Pages:

+ A user can create multiple Pages for a variety of entities.

+ The default privacy setting on Pages is public.

+ Pages cannot +1 other pages on the web (although you do get a +1 button for your Google+ Page).

+ Pages do not have a link to Games (although you can still play them from your personal account profile).

+ Pages doesn't support Hangouts on a mobile device.

+ Pages can display a physical address in the contact details.

So there are some differences between individual profiles and Pages, but they're the sort of things you'd expect from a service that's representing a brand rather than a person. Aside from that, and providing some special sauce you can use to add code to your website, using Google+ Pages is very similar to using your personal account.

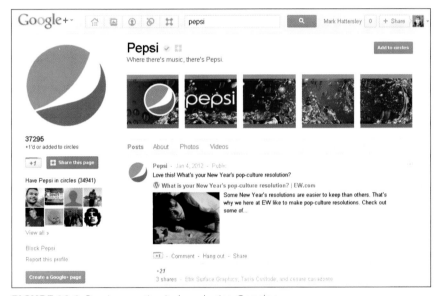

FIGURE 16-1 Pepsi promoting its brand using Google+.

One really great thing about Google+ Pages is that you can use Hangouts in them (as long as you are not working from a mobile device). This enables brand representatives to communicate with up to nine people at a time with the same real-time video chat that you get from your individual account. In other words, you can hang out all day on video chat while your customers come and go, just as you would have many conversations with customers or clients in a physical business environment.

In this sense, it's great for small businesses looking to form intimate connections with their customers. You can post messages, make announcements, show off products with photos and short videos, and chat directly with people.

Creating a Google+ Page

You create a Google+ Page from your own account, so first make sure you're signed in to Google+. Follow these steps to create a Page:

1. **Click Create a Google+ page near the bottom of the right-hand column or visit https://plus.google.com/u/1/pages/create.**

2. **You can choose from five different types of organizations (as shown in Figure 16-2):**

   + Local Business or Place

   + Product or Brand

   + Company, Institution or Organization

   + Arts, Entertainment or Sports

   + Other

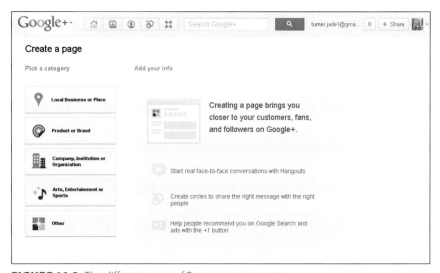

FIGURE 16-2 The different types of Pages you can create.

3. **Choose Product or Brand and type a title into the Page name box.** (The settings for a Local Business or Place are slightly different, and are covered next.)

4. **Type a URL into the Website (optional) box.**

5. **Choose an appropriate content rating using the drop-down list.**
   Here are the options:

   + Any Google+ user

   + Users 18 and older

   + Users 21 and older

   + Alcohol related

6. **Select the I agree to the Pages Terms and I am authorized to create this page check box.**

If you choose Alcohol related or Users 21 and older you currently get a message saying "Our product is not available for you yet. Please come back later."

When setting up a Local Business or Place, you get a slightly different set of options. Follow these steps to create a local business or place:

1. **Click Create a Google+ page.**

2. **Click Local Business or Place.**

3. **Choose the appropriate country from the drop-down list.**

4. **Enter the telephone number for the business or place (it must be listed on Google Maps).**

5. **Click Locate.**

6. **Click the correct business that appears in the list.** If the business is not listed, you need to add it to Google.

7. **Ensure that the basic information is correct (as shown in Figure 16-3).**

8. **Choose a Category.**

9. **Choose an appropriate content rating using the drop-down list. Here are the options:**

   + Any Google+ user

   + Users 18 and older

   + Users 21 and older

   + Alcohol related

10. Select the I agree to the Pages Terms and I am authorized to create this page check box.

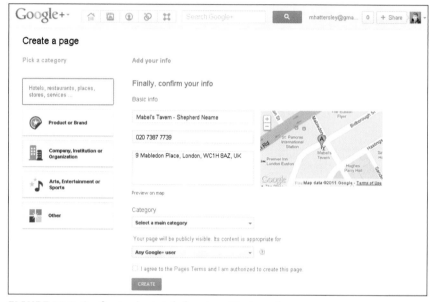

FIGURE 16-3 Confirming basic info for a Local Business Page.

The Page has now been created, although it's fairly sparse at first. Now all comments and notifications you receive will be regarding the Page and not your primary account (click OK at the top of the screen to remove a warning about this).

You can now start to set up your Page's public profile:

1. Type a short (ten words or fewer) description about your Page into the Tagline box (as shown in Figure 16-4).

2. Click Change profile photo and drag a photo to the main area (or click Select a photo from your computer and locate an appropriate image).

3. Click Set as profile photo.

4. Use the drag handles to resize the profile photo and click Set as profile photo again.

5. Click Continue.

FIGURE 16-4 Setting up a Page's public profile.

The final step in the Page setup is to share it with the people in your Circles (the ones in your personal profile):

1. **Click Share on Google+ and then click Share to publicly announce the Page.**

2. **By default, it is shared publicly (as shown in Figure 16-5).** You can remove the Public Circle if you want to share it with a limited group of people.

FIGURE 16-5 Sharing a Google+ Page.

3. **Add a post to go on the Page and click Share.**

4. **Click Finish to create the Page.**

HOW DO I BUILD TRAFFIC TO MY PAGE? Consistently adding good content, sharing other content, and communicating with other people helps. And don't forget to keep sharing the posts on your Page.

CAN I USE GOOGLE+ PAGES ON A MOBILE DEVICE? Not at the moment. You can only use your own profile on a smartphone. But I expect this feature will be included in an update down the line.

Switching between Pages

When you first set up a Page, you will be logged into it and using it instead of your own account. Any of your posts, comments, shares, pictures, and videos are associated with (and come from) the Page you are logged into, instead of your own account.

FIGURE 16-6 Switching between your profile and Pages.

A drop-down list with the Pages associated with your account appears below the account name in the top-left of the screen. Click the drop-down list and choose the Page you want (as shown in Figure 16-6).

CAN MORE THAN ONE PERSON MANAGE A PAGE? Yes. When on your Page, click Settings in the top-right and Managers in the left-hand column. Enter the name of an additional manager and click Invite.

Developing Your Page

When you first start using your Page, you view a page with some hints for getting started, as shown in Figure 16-7 (you only see this page the first time).

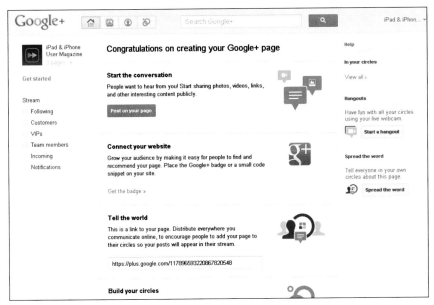

FIGURE 16-7 Welcome to Pages.

The following options are available:

+ **Start the conversation.** This takes you to your Stream so you can create a post.

+ **Connect your website.** This gives you a snippet of code that you can use to create a Google+ badge for your website.

+ **Tell the world.** The text box here contains a web link to your Google+ Page.

+ **Build your circles.** No link appears here, just a reminder that you should use Circles to form links and promote your Page.

+ **Google+ Direct Connect.** If your website qualifies for Direct Connect, you can create a custom Google search that links directly to your Google+ Page. Google+ Direct Connect enables users to search by brands directly from Google+. Click Learn more and How do I make my Google+ Page eligible for Google+ Direct Connect to learn how to apply for Google+ Direct Connect.

+ **Hangouts.** Click the Learn more link to discover how to use Hangouts to communicate with people via your Google+ Page.

+ **+1 Button.** Click the Learn more link to read information on how to integrate +1 with your website.

Once you've done some or all of these things, you can start using your Page just as you would your regular profile.

One thing you should do is flesh out your profile in more detail. A key difference between Pages and your personal profile is that the contact information is more detailed; you can add a physical address, fax number, and other items. Follow these steps:

1. **Click Profile in your Page.**

2. **Click Edit Profile.**

3. **Click How can people reach you and choose from the following options:**

    + Phone

    + Mobile

    + Email

    + Address

    + Fax

    + Pager

    + Chat

4. **Click Address and type your details into the text box (as shown in Figure 16-8).**

FIGURE 16-8 Adding your physical address details.

5. By default, it is shared with Anyone, but you can use the drop-down list to limit who you share your contact details with.

6. Click Save and Done editing.

Connecting Your Page and Website

Typically when you set up a Page, you have a corresponding website, which also promotes your brand. You may want to use Google+ to promote your website.

If this is the case, you should forge links between your Google+ Page and your website. First of all, you should make sure that your URL is listed in your profile, although this is a fairly low-key link and won't (by itself) generate much traffic. (Obviously, creating posts about your website in the Stream is also a means of creating traffic.)

You should also use Google's website tools to build your Google+ audience. Follow these steps to connect your website to Google+:

1. Make sure you are using Google+ as your Page and click Get started in the left-hand column.

2. Click Get the badge under the Connect your website section. By default, you won't need to change the Set your Google+ page link (as it already links to your Page).

3. You can change the style of the badge in the Choose your style and preview section. The box in the gray area displays how your badge will look (as shown in Figure 16-9). Choose from the following:

   + Standard badge

   + Small badge

   + Small icon

   + Medium icon

   + Large icon

   + No badge

4. Use the Language drop-down list to change the language (if you want another language than English (US)).

5. **Leave the asynchronous check box selected.** This speeds up tracking of your site in Google Analytics.

6. **If you are creating a HTML5 valid website, select the HTML5 valid syntax check box.**

7. **Leave the Parse setting on Default.** If you choose Explicit, you need to implement a JavaScript call manually.

8. **The code appears in a text box at the end of the page.** Cut the first part of the code to the `<head>` of your web page and the second part in the place where you want the badge.

FIGURE 16-9 Choose a style and preview for your badge.

Setting Up Direct Connect

Direct Connect is a feature in Google Search that enables people to search for your brand's Google+ Page. They do this by typing a + symbol and the name of your brand, so if they type **+pepsi,** Google returns the Google+ Page at the top of the suggested search options (as shown in Figure 16-10). If you type **+pepsi** into Google Search and press Enter or Return, you are taken straight to the Google+ Page.

FIGURE 16-10 A Direct Connect result for a search.

Setting up Direct Connect requires you to add a piece of code to your web page. The next time Google Search crawls your site, it adds the Direct Connect details to Google Search.

Follow these steps to set up Direct Connect:

1. **Visit https://developers.google.com/+/plugins/badge.**

2. **Copy the Direct Connect code from the text box (as shown in Figure 16-11).**

3. **Paste the code into the `<head>` area of your website.**

It may take a while for Google to crawl your website and the Direct Connect link to work.

Direct Connect

Google+ Direct Connect helps visitors find your Google+ page and add it to their circles from directly within Google Search. Once you've created your Google+ page, finish connecting it to your site by adding the following code inside the `<head>` element of your site:

```
<link href="https://plus.google.com/{plusPageUrl}" rel="publisher" />
```

You can also connect your site by simply linking to your Google+ page anywhere on the page using a standard `<a>` element. Just make sure to include the `rel="publisher"` attribute on the link. For example, see the static Google+ badge.

FIGURE 16-11 Include this code in your website for Direct Connect.

Related Questions

+ How do I fill out my Google+ Page profile? **CHAPTER 2, Completing Your Google+ Profile**

+ How do I get followers for my Page? **CHAPTER 4, Finding Friends from Your Contacts**

+ How do I create activity on my Page? **CHAPTER 6, Creating a Post to Share in Your Stream**

+ How do I have live chats with people? **CHAPTER 7, Discovering What Hangouts Are All About**

APPENDIX: RESOURCES

Even though Google+ is a relatively new social media service, you can find a lot of tools, websites, and blogs to help you make the most of it. Here are some resources that will help you maximize Google+.

Setting Up

An important aspect you should not overlook when setting up a Google account is picking, creating, and, most important, remembering a strong password. You must also consider marketing, promoting, and (for a business) branding. Here are some tools that can help you.

MICROSOFT SAFETY & SECURITY CENTER

www.microsoft.com/security/online-privacy/passwords-create.aspx

This site has some good advice on creating strong passwords.

STRONG PASSWORD GENERATOR

http://strongpasswordgenerator.com

If you draw a blank when trying to come up with passwords, try this web service. It suggests strong passwords and memorable phrases to help you remember the character combinations.

ARE YOU A SOCIAL MEDIA BEGINNER? BEGIN HERE

www.searchenginepeople.com/blog/social-media-beginner-howto.html

If you're thinking of Google+ in business terms, such as using it to promote your own small business or your company's larger brand, this article by Gabriella Sannino, an SEO and copyrighting specialist who owns Level43.com, has good pointers to get you started.

5 STEPS TO BRANDING YOUR SOCIAL MEDIA PROFILES

www.brandingrevolution.com/branding/5-steps-to-branding-your-social-media-profiles

Even if you're not working for a megacorporation or setting up your own brand, this post from the blog Branding Revolution has some great advice for setting up consistent profiles across various social media sites.

Marketplaces

One great trick to making the most of any social media platform is to install apps and browser extensions. I mention a lot of them throughout the book, and new and better ones come along every day. Here's where you'll find the best apps and extensions for Google+.

GOOGLE PLAY

https://play.google.com

Along with the official Google+ app for Android, this Google site includes a wealth of Android apps that expand your social media experience. In Google Play, click Apps, click Categories, and then click Social to find all the latest apps designed to improve your mobile social experience.

ITUNES STORE
http://itunes.apple.com

iOS users can find a massive list of social networking apps in the iTunes Store. Open iTunes and click iTunes Store in the left-hand column. Click App Store and, in the right-hand column, choose Social Networking from the drop-down list. This takes you to even more information, including Top Charts, What's Hot, and New.

CHROME WEB STORE
https://chrome.google.com/webstore

The wealth of apps and extensions for the Google Chrome browser on this site are designed to help you work with social media sites (including Google+). Open the Chrome Web Store and click Extensions. Then click Social & Communication in the left-hand column under Extensions to view all the latest social media extensions.

Finding People on Google+

When your profile is set up, it's time to reach out and find people. While Google's built-in search tool is a great way to fill in your Circles, you can also use some dedicated directories and lists when you're looking for specific types of people (for example, photographers, engineers, journalists, and so on).

POPULAR LISTS ON GOOGLE+ COUNTER
http://gpc.fm

This site has user-curated lists. You can add yourself to a list or even start your own list.

GOOGLE+ DIRECTORY

www.gglpls.com

This is a large directory of Google+ users, sorted by tags and location (plus the number of followers and friends). You can add yourself to the list.

UNOFFICIAL GOOGLE+ RECOMMENDED USERS

www.recommendedusers.com

Rather than presenting a huge list of Google+ users, this directory focuses on quality and recommends influential people (bloggers, podcasters, authors, women in tech, and so on) that you can add to your Circles.

GOOGLE+ SEARCH

http://gplussearch.com

This is a customized search engine that can return results from Google+ posts and profiles, and Google Reader. If you're looking for high-profile subjects in your area who are a little obscure for the standard lists, this is a good way to find them.

Marketing Your Google+ Page

When you have set up your Google+ account and populated your Circles, you'll want to start promoting and managing your page, as well as use it to promote any brands you might have. Keep these pointers in mind.

GOOGLE+ SUPPORT SITE

http://support.google.com/plus

The +1 service is central to Google's goal to socialize all content (including yours) on the web. There's a wealth of information about it on this Google+ support site. On the support site, click About the +1 button underneath Get started in the left-hand column.

GOOGLE+ SOCIAL STATISTICS
http://socialstatistics.com

This site enables you to track detailed statistics about your Google+ page, as well as the pages of other registered users.

TOPRANK
www.toprankblog.com

This online marketing blog is designed to help small businesses make the most of social media.

THE BRANDBUILDER BLOG
http://thebrandbuilder.wordpress.com

This blog provides great advice about turning your social media endeavors into a strong brand.

Reading Up on Social Media Developments

One of the best ways to stay on top of Google+ developments (and social media in general) is to read some of the better blogs. There's a lot of bad advice on social media and even more regarding search engine optimization. Here are some sites that will help you separate good ideas from bad ones.

SEARCH ENGINE JOURNAL
www.searchenginejournal.com

This is a good site for picking up tips on promoting pages and websites in general.

THE OFFICIAL GOOGLE BLOG

http://googleblog.blogspot.com

This blog gives you information on Google developments straight from the horse's mouth.

MASHABLE

http://mashable.com

For a daily entertaining read on developments in the world of social media, check out this site.

THE ANTI-SOCIAL MEDIA BLOG

http://theantisocialmedia.com

Finally, if all this business with social media is making your head hurt, head over to a blog with an array of badly scrawled satiric cartoons.

Following Interesting People

With millions of people on Google+, it may seem foolish to suggest you follow just a few individuals. Aside from the litany of sports and pop stars, here are some of the most influential movers and shakers in the world of social media.

BRIAN SOLIS

This industry analyst and entrepreneur shares some of the most thoughtful posts on social media developments.

JASON FALLS

Here you'll find an entertaining daily Google+ account from the CEO of Social Media Explorer.

LARRY PAGE

Google CEO and cofounder isn't a prolific Google+ poster, but his posts are always regarding high-profile developments in Google and are worth following.

SERGEY BRIN

Google's other CEO and cofounder is a more prolific poster (and quite a good photographer). Follow him to read some interesting thoughts from a very influential person.

BRADLEY HOROWITZ

As you'd expect, Google's vice president of the Google+ product is a prolific poster and has some good thoughts on why Google+ is the way it is.

VIC GUNDOTRA

The senior vice president of engineering at Google has some great advice on how to get the most out of the social network.

NATALIE VILLALOBOS

Google+'s community manager shares the best posts from the rest of the Google team. Adding her to your Circles is a good way to get a collection of information about the decisions Google is making.

✛ INDEX

The Genius is in.

iPad 2
PORTABLE GENIUS
Second Edition

978-1-118-17303-9

iPhone 4S
PORTABLE GENIUS
Also covers iPhone 4!

978-1-118-09384-9

iPod & iTunes
PORTABLE GENIUS
Second Edition

978-0-470-64351-8

MacBook Air
PORTABLE GENIUS
Third Edition

978-1-118-18618-3

MacBook Pro
PORTABLE GENIUS
Third Edition

978-0-470-64204-7

Macs
PORTABLE GENIUS
Third Edition

978-1-118-16433-4

iMac
PORTABLE GENIUS

978-1-118-14758-0

Mac OS X Lion
PORTABLE GENIUS

978-1-118-02239-9

iLife '11
PORTABLE GENIUS

978-0-470-64348-8

Aperture 3
PORTABLE GENIUS

978-0-470-38672-9

Microsoft Office for Mac 2011
PORTABLE GENIUS

978-0-470-61019-0

The essentials for every forward-thinking Apple user are now available on the go. Designed for easy access to tools and shortcuts, the *Portable Genius* series has all the information you need to maximize your digital lifestyle. With a full-color interior and easy-to-navigate content, the *Portable Genius* series offers innovative tips and tricks as well as savvy advice that will save you time and increase your productivity.

e **Available in print and e-book formats.**

WILEY
Now you know